TESTIMONY:

10 STORIES DETAILING SUPERNATURAL MIRACLES, BLESSINGS, and
THE POWER OF PRAYER

I0133206

A.C. Ross

TESTIMONY:

10 STORIES DETAILING SUPERNATURAL MIRACLES, BLESSINGS, and
THE POWER OF PRAYER

By A.C. Ross

A.C. Ross

ISBN: 978-0-9904430-0-1.

TESTIMONY:

10 STORIES DETAILING SUPERNATURAL MIRACLES, BLESSINGS, and
THE POWER OF PRAYER

By A.C. Ross

To my sons,

My walking, talking,
supernatural blessings from God.

--Love,
Mommy

A.C. Ross

Preface

My, oh my, how times have changed.

Children – young and innocent - are abused, raped, and murdered. Young women, once valued, their honor once protected, are now sexualized, objectified, and disrespected.

Young mothers have been abandoned. They, often alone, are responsible for turning young boys into men and young girls into women, when they are barely women themselves. Yet, they must bear the responsibility because young fathers are absent.

Men, even mere boys, are shot down in the streets, in their homes, or are locked up and thrown away. Their lives, seemingly, have no value.

Elderly women – grandmothers, for heaven's sake - are raped and robbed in their own homes. Elderly men fare no better. Some are beaten up, just because. Even worse, many times these assaults occur from the hands of the young men who used to look up to the elders. The same young people who, more often than not, are shot down in the streets by their own peers...and so the cycle of hurt, violence, anger, and loss continues. It has become second nature, as common as the seasons changing.

If you are like me you have wondered, *What is happening to this world, our world? Where is our safe place?*

All of us are affected, yet some of us do nothing. We either don't care, don't care enough, or don't know what to do.

Others of us look for solutions. We look to our communities, only to find that some of our very neighbors are responsible for the monstrosities – the senseless crimes - that occur.

Our neighbors, some that are revered community leaders, are the abusers of our children, or they look the other way while they are being abused.

We look to the church, but it doesn't appear to be much different from the rest of the world. In what used to be our refuge – the church - we are finding pastors having sexual relationships with the very youth they are supposed to serve, the youth they are supposed to inspire. Seemingly, our children are as safe in the "house of the Lord", as they are on the street.

We know that things need to change, but we don't know where to turn.

We feel sorry for the youth of today – losing their lives, taking others' lives, going nowhere fast.

We feel sorry for women – young and old – who have been taught to use their bodies to get ahead, because the world rewards them when they do.

We feel sorry for the elders because they no longer receive the respect they deserve. They are not able to impart their years of hard-earned wisdom, because no one listens to them anymore.

We feel sorry for ourselves, ashamed even, that we are unable, unwilling, maybe even afraid to speak up when we see things that need to be changed, behaviors that need to be corrected, and guidance that needs to be given. We don't speak up, and many times we have been bullied into accepting beliefs that are not our own, that go against what we know and believe to be right and true.

Perhaps most of all we feel sorry for our children, fearful of the kind of world they will grow up in.

I have sometimes wondered where God is in all that is happening. Perhaps you have too. You, like I, may have wondered if we are all alone in this world, without His love, grace, and mercy. Are we in a present day Sodom and Gomorrah, or in such a time and place as where Noah lived when given the news that the world would be destroyed?

With jobs lost every day, so many living in poverty, families losing their homes, hunger and disease prevalent - in all of this suffering and amongst so much lack - you may have questioned whether blessings still exist? You may have questioned if miracles are still happening, or if such "miraculous occurrences" are things of the past? You may wonder if miracles are nothing more than fallacies relegated to Old Testament bible chapters and childhood fairytales?

Well, I am here to tell you, and _**show**_ you - with actual proof - that blessings and miracles do still exist.

I, and many others, are living proof that prayer holds an awesome power and is able to deliver God's love, mercy, kindness, grace, and favor – to your job, your children, your home, your spouse, your community, our world. We are not alone in these times of loss, suffering, and lack.

And what better time than now to remember what can happen when prayer goes up?

For those of you who don't know, or may have forgotten, when prayer goes up blessings do (still) come down.

This book was inspired by God – indeed requested by Him – to encourage, remind, illustrate, and boldly declare that God is still in the blessing business. He is still creating miracles. And He is as powerful today as He was in biblical times.

Whether you are facing illness, danger, death, loss, financial struggles, family problems, declining faith, or the seemingly impossible - there is nothing too hard for God.

Many of us treat God like a rewards card.

A rewards card allows us to store up points to cash in for something special at a later date. We can use our points for a pizza, a free flight, or even a vacation. The more "points" we accumulate, the bigger the prize we can receive at a later date.

But God is not like that. We don't have to be good for a long time, and do so many good deeds to store up so many points to use toward a future blessing. God is ready to bless us right now. It doesn't matter if we have been saved a decade, a year, a month, or an hour. Even if we haven't been saved and are merely contemplating it, He is a God of second chances, blessings, grace, mercy, love, favor.

He is still – currently, right now, today – moving mountains, though today those mountains may look like debt, divorce, a troubled child, a foreclosed home, a dangerous alley, a dire circumstance. He is still blessing people and circumstances, healing diseases, and defying diagnoses. He is still performing miracles.

I pray as you read these stories that you are reminded of God's goodness, and His power. I hope this book launches a Prayer Movement, and that as prayer is resurrected, we start to see things change. Lives change.

My prayer is that as we pray we begin to see children protected, women loved and cherished, men taking their rightful places as "heads and not tails", elders respected.

I pray families are strengthened, marriages revived, and that opportunities begin to abound that bring forth prosperity and healing.

God is still in business. Just read on to see what He's been up to...

Testimony 1: God Sends Assurance and Cures Breast Cancer

My family and I have always been very close. We went bike-riding every Sunday after church, had water balloon fights around the yard (girls vs. boys) and took fishing and "crabbing" trips.

If we were going fishing, us children would go in the backyard, before the sun rose, to catch our bait, while my mom (and maternal grandmother if she was accompanying us) packed our breakfasts and lunch, and my dad loaded up the car with the poles, tackle boxes, bottled waters, nets, and all the other fishing gear.

If we were going crabbing, it was even better.

Growing up in New Orleans, "going crabbing" is as common as having red beans and rice or gumbo for dinner. Crabbing is when you "fish" for crabs. Unlike fishing, however, crabbing involves a lot more work and discipline.

To crab, you must first have a location that is isolated, remote, and swampy. This of course, is prime environment for snakes and alligators. As a young girl I was never scared, however, because I knew my dad would never let any harm come to us.

Secondly, to crab you must have your bait. In our case, bait was turkey necks tied to thick string. You also needed sticks. These sticks would serve as the stakes in the ground from which the "crabbing" traps would be launched.

When we were going crabbing, we would head out at about 4:30 a.m. to begin the drive to our location. When we got there, my dad and brothers (and uncles and cousins, if they were coming along) would search the area for the prime spot, and when they found it they would set the "stakes" (sticks) around the perimeter of the water, in the shallow part.

While they were looking for an ideal crabbing spot, the girls (my mom and I, sometimes also grandmothers, aunts, and cousins) would get the bait ready, which involved tying the string around the turkey necks.

When that was done, and the locations were ready, we would tie the other end of the strings around the stakes in the ground, leaving enough slack in the string so that when the crabs would swim to the water's edge to grab the bait, the line would grow taut, informing us that a crab was on the line. And that is where the real work, and the real fun, began!

To reel the crabs in, you had to be patient, slow, and methodical. Because there were no hooks to hook the crab on, and thus they could easily let go of the meat and simply swim away and back into the deeper water, you had to very slowly draw "the line" back towards you and your waiting net, without the crab feeling the movement and becoming aware that you were moving them towards the water's edge and into the perimeter of the net.

By it being so early in the morning, the day would be so quiet and still. The only sounds we'd hear would be an occasional ripple of water as a turtle (or something else?!) peeked its head out of, and back into, the water.

When you had "walked" the crab towards the shallow end of the water and over your net (which was always placed below the line and far enough into the water so that the crab couldn't see it) you were to then scoop up the net thereby scooping up the crab. And viola!, you had caught a crab!

If you were lucky, because of how crabs hang onto each other, you might have caught two crabs! And boy would we celebrate! Unless another crab was on another line, we would whoop and holler and scream and dance. Then we'd quiet down again, and prepare to catch another crab, then another.

When it was all said and done, and we'd caught a few dozen crabs, we would go home, bathe, cook the crabs, then have a get together with family and friends, laughing, eating, playing games, and enjoying each other's company.

Laughing, eating, playing games, and enjoying each other's company just about sums up how I spent my childhood. It was a childhood to remember, and I wouldn't change a thing.

My immediate family consisted of my dad and mom (who were high school sweethearts), an older brother, myself (the only girl) and my younger brother.

My brothers and I all went to the same elementary school together, and everyone knew our family. As we got older, our house became the place where all the neighborhood children and our cousins hung out – either playing video games in our living room, basketball in our backyard, see-sawing on the seesaw that my daddy had built, or riding go-carts at the local high school's running track. We always had good times. But that all changed one day.

When I turned 12, my parents split up, and my brothers and I were shook to our core[1]. We hadn't seen it coming. One day we were a family, living together, and the next day we had two households.

To say it was a difficult time is an understatement, but with the help of family, and with the prayers of our grandmothers, we got through it. Sometimes worse for wear, but we got through it.

During the time of my parents' divorce, I first learned the power of prayer. Those days were the hardest of my young life. Even though I had always known about prayer – God, church, and prayer had been a part of my family for generations – I had never had a personal relationship with God. I was baptized simply when I was old enough to. I went to church because that was what was expected. I prayed because I had always prayed, and because my parents made sure we did.

During that time, however, I became a prayer warrior, thanks in great part to my paternal grandmother, Florence. And I remain a prayer

[1] See Testimony #10.

warrior today, thanks in great part to my maternal grandmother, Evelyn. The pain didn't go away right away, and my parents never got back together, but by the time I was 15 I was back on track, had started a prayer group with some family and friends, was on scholarship to a private school, was tithing 10% (at least) of my paycheck from my first job to my church, and was doing great.

God had healed me, had softened my heart (no more fighting for me), had given me peace during a chaotic time, and most importantly, had cemented my belief that He could do all things. And that prayer worked.

Fast forward three years.

It was the year 2000, and I was on my way to college. I had been awarded a full academic scholarship to an out-of-town school, and was geared up and ready to go.

During my first semester of college, despite being away on my own for the first time in my life, and despite being at a certified "party school" I made a 4.0 and was put on the President's List, which was the University's highest honor.

At the end of my first semester of college, my mom was diagnosed with Breast Cancer. She didn't tell my brothers and me right away because she didn't want to ruin our Christmas. She waited until December 26th (6 days after she had found out) and told us the horrible news.

My older brother said nothing. He simply clammed up and shut down. He walked out of the room and left the house, undoubtedly to process this dreadful news alone.

My little brother, 12 at the time, immediately began to cry. He didn't understand it, and yet he understood all too well the implications. He knew, as did I, that people died of this disease. I didn't cry, however. At least not right then.

Eighteen then, what I did instead was intellectualize the situation. I asked all the right questions: *What stage was the Breast Cancer in? What did the doctors say? Where do we go from here, as it concerns treatment?*

I began to reassure her. I was trying to be strong for my mom who is also extremely strong and, not surprisingly, showed no emotion. I said that everything was going to be fine. I said we'd get through this. I said a lot of things that I didn't know if I necessarily believed.

I said all the right things, hugged my mom (I mean, really held her!), then I went downstairs into my room, dropped the facade and cried my heart out. I was so distraught! At that time, I could not imagine a life that would not include my mom. At the age of 18, my thought was, if my mom wasn't here, then I didn't want to be, plain and simple.

As I was crying, an apparition appeared.

Now keep in mind that this is a true story. I am not making any of this up, or enhancing any of it for anyone's benefit. This is truly how God moved in my (and my family's) life.

I saw this apparition. It had no face, only a presence, but the peace it put in my heart, even during this time of turmoil, let me know that it was an angel. I was sure of it. And still am.

The angel spoke. It said, "YOUR MOM IS GOING TO BE FINE." Then it disappeared, as easily as it had appeared. I was astounded! Truly amazed!

I bolted out of my room, ran upstairs (in tears) telling my mom and little brother what had just happened. God had sent an angel, who stood before me, right there in my bedroom, and reassured me, so that I could reassure my family that everything was going to be okay.

My older brother, 21 at the time, took it the hardest. And in silence. He simply got mad at the world. But when he got back to the house, and I told him of what I had seen, it seemed to put him at ease. It gave him peace. Peace that we would soon all need.

My mom got worse before she got better.

I was home for Christmas vacation when she told us. But I was living away from home in college. When I went back to school, I couldn't concentrate and I called home constantly. Most of the time my mom's condition had worsened, and she was hospitalized almost constantly.

She'd started chemotherapy and had lost weight and all of her hair. She no longer resembled the strong, vivacious, independent woman I had known all my life. She was now this weak, sick, frail woman.

I resigned from school (without telling my parents what I was going to do because I knew what they would say). My mom was my priority. I went home to take care of her.

I often questioned God about His promise that my mom would be okay. I knew that God wouldn't lie, yet I looked at my mom losing her battle with Cancer. But God did not lie. He is not a man, that He should lie[2] (Numbers 23:19).

My mom eventually got better, completely better. By the grace of God, she fought her battle with Cancer and won. By 2005, she was in remission, and was quite possibly even healthier and more vivacious than before the Cancer diagnosis!

Once she was healthy, I went back to school, and even though I had resigned and sat out of school for two semesters, I managed to graduate from college within four years, and with honors!

That's how good God is!

He not only healed my mom, but He sent His reassurance to my family, through little old me, so that we'd know throughout it all that He was there with us.

---

[2] This scripture means that God does not lie like people do.

And even with all that, as if that was not enough,
He went on to make a way for me to finish school,
on time, and with honors.

It is now nearly 2013. I finished my Ph.D. a year
ago, am happily married to a man of God, and we
have two beautiful sons. My message is this: Prayer
works. Trust and rely on God.

He delivers.

Testimony 2: God Defies a Doctor's Diagnosis

My son actually knew we were pregnant before we did.

He was three years old, and would come up to me and say, "Mommy, the baby's hungry." Or he'd say, "Mommy, I'm talking to my baby sister," while leaning in to whisper to my stomach. I would look at my husband and say, "What baby is he talking about?" And my husband would shrug. Or my husband would look at me, expectantly, and I would say, "No news here."

Even though my husband and I had recently (2 months prior) started trying for baby number two, we didn't think we could get pregnant so soon. I had just gotten off a pretty invasive form of birth control, and the doctor had told me that it would take at least six months for my menstrual cycle to return, and about 12-18 months before we would get pregnant. So a pregnancy, only two months after getting off birth control, was not expected.

One night, after my three year old had a pretty animated conversation with my tummy while I was putting him to bed, I decided right then and there to take the leftover pregnancy test that had been at the bottom of our bathroom cabinet.

My husband had just left a few hours prior for a five-day business trip and I had been cleaning out the bathroom cabinet as I packed up that particular bathroom (we were moving out-of-state within the month), and that's where I had noticed the leftover pregnancy test.

I took the test, lay it on the bathroom counter, and forgot about it as I went back to packing. When I was done packing the bathroom I moved on to the laundry room, all the while chit-chatting on the phone with my best friend.

When I went back into the bathroom to pack something from the laundry room into one of the bathroom boxes, I noticed the pregnancy test that I'd forgotten about and leaned over to check it.

I saw that it had a faint pink line (indicating pregnancy). The line was so faint, however, that I questioned its legitimacy. I thought I was imagining the pink line or that because it was so faint it wasn't valid. Still, I was stunned.

I whispered to my friend, "Oh my God! Girl, there is a line there. It's faint, but it's there." She whispered back, "What are you talking about?" (I hadn't told her - or my husband for that matter - that I was even taking a pregnancy test). I whispered to her, while slowly backing away from the pregnancy test, "I took a pregnancy test and there's a line there, but it's super faint."

Don't ask me why, but we whispered the whole conversation.

My best friend told me, "If you want to be sure, go get a digital pregnancy test, that way it will definitely say either yes or no." I thought that was a great idea! So even though it was nighttime (about 8 p.m.), I picked my three year old up out of his bed, while still in his pajamas, and drove a few blocks to the drugstore to purchase a pregnancy test.

This time I stood there the entire time it took for the test to work. Sure enough, within a couple minutes, the digital pregnancy test read "Yes".

I blinked a few times in an effort to process it all, because it had happened so quickly. I mean, just a couple months before, the doctor had told me we wouldn't get pregnant so soon. Then I smiled. And I giggled. I did a little twirl in the bathroom and thanked God for our newest little one.

By the time I had finished my happy dance and praise of God, my husband called to let me know that he had safely landed. I tried with everything I could to conceal the joy in my voice. Since Father's Day was that Sunday (two days after my husband would return home from his business trip), I had decided that I would tell him then.

My husband and I stayed on the phone, chatting it up while he caught a cab to his hotel, checked in, then ordered room service, and all the while he had no idea that I was carrying our newest little one. The joy I felt was so palpable that I just knew my husband would sense it, or smell it, or even hear it in my voice, so I decided to get off the phone. We said our "I love yous" and our "good nights", and got off the phone. I lay in bed talking to God and to our newest little one until I fell asleep.

The next day I went to the doctor's office and had an official pregnancy test. My pregnancy was confirmed, but I was also told that it was incredibly early (my hCG levels were really low[3]) so I would have to be retested in two days.

---

[3] Human Chorionic Gonadotropin (hCG) is a hormone made by the cells that form the placenta during pregnancy. At-home pregnancy tests use traces of the hCG hormone found in urine to indicate pregnancy, and it can also be used in a medical

In the meantime I bought no less than four more tests and took two per day. I took one in the morning and one at night, and sure enough with each passing day that line grew deeper and pinker and showed up quicker.

When I went back to the doctor's office for my follow-up test to check my hCG levels, they had doubled and I was confirmed pregnant by the same doctor who had told me that I wouldn't get pregnant so soon. I went home to bask in my pregnancy, all while trying to keep the secret from my husband for the next few days.

When my hubby came home, Father's Day was still two days away, so I had to continue to keep my secret. Finally Sunday, June 19, 2011 came around and after church we went out to eat. I had wrapped a pair of baby booties in a gift box and had a card that said "There's a new pea in our pod." I couldn't even wait until the food arrived before I gave my husband his "gifts."

The first one was a cute little card from our three year old and the next "gift" was the news of our pregnancy. When my husband opened the "There's

setting to determine if a pregnancy is progressing appropriately, by drawing blood and analyzing whether the hCG levels are increasing.

a new pea in our pod" card, he read it, looked at me, and then read it again. All the while I am looking at him, darn near brimming over with excitement, waiting for him to "catch on." A few seconds later he got it and half-exclaimed, half-asked "We're having a baby?!"

The whole restaurant heard, at least those sitting in our section. I shrieked, "Yes!" And everyone started to clap for us while my husband hugged and kissed me, hugged our son and started to call family and friends. I don't even think he ate the food he ordered. He was too busy calling everyone to tell them the good news!

The next month or so passed seemingly quickly because we were all so busy. I was in the last year of finishing up my Ph.D., and my husband was working at a satellite location.

Since we were all planning to relocate back to the main office, we were packing up our home to move the several hundred miles away. And I was so tired! I had packing to do and a dissertation to complete, but all I wanted to do was sleep. Tiredness was normal, so I didn't complain. I was actually grateful that at least I hadn't had morning sickness as bad as I had experienced with my first son.

Within a few months, however, I started to think something was wrong. Although I had lost a pound a week during my first month of pregnancy, I quickly made up for that weight loss. I got really big and swollen very quickly, despite a limited diet.

It also didn't help that at my first ultrasound they couldn't find the baby, and later told me it was because it was smaller than they had estimated, leading them to believe that I wasn't as far along as they'd originally thought. But even though my baby was small and I wasn't as far along as originally thought, based on my size, I looked much farther along than I should have. I was barely four months pregnant and looked as if I was already eight months.

Being a researcher, I looked up what could be the possible culprit – what could be causing me to gain so much weight so rapidly - and I kept coming up with preeclampsia.

Preeclampsia is a medical condition characterized by increased blood pressure and protein in the urine, caused by kidney problems. It affects the placenta, and can affect the mother's kidney, liver, and brain. When preeclampsia causes seizures, the condition is known as eclampsia.

When I brought up my concerns to my doctors, they dismissed them because I did not have certain symptoms, such as protein in my urine or high blood pressure. So I dismissed my concerns too.

Yet, I kept getting more and more swollen. It got to a point where my hands were so swollen that I could barely close them around my toothbrush. And my feet were so swollen that my husband could poke them and leave a fingerprint.

At almost every appointment I went to I raised a concern about my weight gain (20 pounds in the second month, about 10 pounds in the third and fourth months, 15 pounds in the fifth month and 10 pounds in the sixth month) and I was always told the same thing – "you're fine." The doctors would explain that my weight gain was more than it should be, but that it was not a problem, and that I was not suffering from preeclampsia.

It also didn't help that I'd had doctors across two states because I'd had to travel to a different state for my dissertation meetings.

I successfully defended my dissertation near my sixth month of pregnancy. All the years of hard work had finally paid off! I had become a doctor!

Within the next month, my husband, son, and I bought a home and we moved in the day before Thanksgiving. We spent Thanksgiving Day eating on top of boxes, but were thankful God had blessed us with a new home.

That night I wasn't feeling well so we called the doctor and she told us what to do. I went back to bed and the next day the doctor called me back to personally check on me. I had not been seen by this particular doctor before and I thought that was incredibly thoughtful of her to call and personally check on me. I told her I was better, and we got off the phone.

Two days later I wasn't feeling well again. This time I was in tears. And I am not a crier. Still, I did not want to call the doctor's office because I knew they would just tell me to do such and such and we'd get off the phone. I finally confided in my husband that I was in pain (there was a knot at the top of my stomach, and I was feeling constipated and nauseated all at the same time). My husband insisted that we call the doctor and this time they told us to come in.

On the way to the hospital the bumps in the road were excruciating – they felt like they were jarring that knot that was sitting at the top of my stomach

- and I was full-blown crying. I entered the emergency room bent over in pain and was so uncomfortable that the Triage nurse could not check me in while in the designated area. The doctor and nurses on-call led me into a room and let me lie down, while they proceeded to run a number of tests on me, in an effort to figure out what was going on.

By the way, although I was only six months pregnant by then (exactly 27 weeks, 3 days) I had already gained 60 pounds. Initially the on-call Obstetrician thought I was constipated (based on what I'd reported) and she gave me a laxative. I threw up and actually started to feel better to the point where the doctor had begun preparing my discharge papers.

And then the pain returned - with a vengeance.

My blood pressure soared and all of a sudden the issue became life or death. More blood was drawn, my blood pressure got into the 200s (220/120) and the pain had me screaming out, begging for medication, despite the fact that during my pregnancy I did not take medicine for anything.

The doctor and nurse tried everything to lower my blood pressure, including continually shifting me right to left. The diagnoses ranged from gall bladder infection to possible preeclampsia. When I heard the word preeclampsia something inside of me clicked, because I had suspected preeclampsia at several points throughout my pregnancy.

Sure enough, it was confirmed. Not only did I have preeclampsia, I had severe preeclampsia - HELLP Syndrome[4] - and was told that it was a life-threatening situation that would require the doctors to remove my baby immediately. The exact words were "We're preparing you for an emergency C-section, and we'll be taking the baby in 45 minutes."

I was surprisingly calm. And calm is not my persona (I am a worry-wart). I asked if it was absolutely necessary that they take my baby out so soon (three months before the baby was due). They told me that was the only way to save my life and that of my baby, or else I could develop eclampsia, have a seizure, and die. I asked about my baby's health, as that was all I was thinking about, and was allowed to speak to the Neonatologists on call. The

---

[4] HELLP Syndrome is a rare, life-threatening form of severe preeclampsia in which 1 or 2 out of every 1,000 pregnant women develops hemolysis (H), a breakdown of red blood cells, (EL) elevated liver enzymes, and (LP) low platelet count (www.ncbi.nlm.nih.gov/pubmedhealth/PMH0001892/).

Neonatologist, they told me, would let me know what to expect for my baby.

A Neonatologist is a medical doctor trained to handle the most complex and high-risk medical problems in newborn babies, such as prematurity, serious illnesses, sicknesses, and birth defects. There were two Neonatologists - one ending a shift and one coming on – and both told me what to expect for my preterm (premature) baby.

The Neonatologists said that by our baby being born three months early, "it[5]" would have breathing problems and would be on a ventilator, that the baby would be in an incubator, and would have to stay in the Neonatal Intensive Care Unit (NICU) for several months, most likely even past "it's" due date, as the baby fought to catch up and battle the disadvantages inherent in being a preemie. This is what we were told to expect.

To say we had not been prepared is an understatement. Both my husband's and my cell phones were dead (we hadn't expected to be admitted to the hospital, and had not grabbed our chargers), and we actually had to use the nurses' phones to call our families and tell them this

---

[5] We hadn't yet told anyone the baby's sex.

horrific news. Our three year old was with us in the hospital, sleeping on the sofa in my hospital room as they prepped me for emergency surgery, because there was no family around to watch him.

Surprisingly though, through all this frenzy, there was no fear. Even as I write this, I am taken back to that place and time and am emotional as I realize the full extent of God's grace and mercy. He truly gave us a peace that surpassed all understanding (Philippians 4:7). Even now, I don't quite fully comprehend how we were able to maintain peace as we sat there awaiting an emergency C-section that would deliver our baby three months earlier than "it" should have been born.

With the nurses' phones in hand we called our family and asked for prayer. My maternal grandmother, Evelyn, is a prayer warrior and we asked her to pray for us. By the time the prayer requests started, all in all, we had whole churches praying for us (my mom called her pastor, my grandmother called hers as well, as well as her prayer partners, and they all began to pray).

We had parents, siblings, aunts, uncles, friends, nurses, and doctors praying for us. And I said a heartfelt prayer of my own. I distinctly remember asking God to post his angels above, below, before, behind, and on either side of that emergency room, that surgery room, and my child's incubator. I asked Him to bless my child and let my child be healthy. I asked Him to bestow His love, grace, and mercy on my child and let my child's life be a testimony. And off we went to surgery.

We had arrived at the hospital on a Saturday night, and after about 12 hours, and countless tests and close calls, my son was born the next morning weighing 1 lb, 11.7 oz, and 13 inches long. He was even smaller than expected, but when they removed him, he let out such a powerful cry that I asked, "Was that my baby?" And the reply was, "Yes, he's a strong little fella!"

I saw my new baby boy briefly, and then he was whisked to the NICU for evaluation, with my husband in tow.

Despite warnings of ventilators, they never happened. We never needed them. Our son, with a birth weight of 788 grams, never had to use a ventilator. And although the doctors commented that he was even smaller than they thought he'd be, he was stronger than any of us could've imagined.

Across the way from the NICU and down the hall, I was also hospitalized. I stayed in the hospital for eight days as the doctors fought to lower my blood pressure, and get my blood levels normalized. They tried one medicinal cocktail then another, all to no avail, as my blood pressure remained dangerously high (despite being prescribed magnesium sulfate, my doctors thought a seizure was imminent). But I didn't complain, because I was happy that I got to stay in the hospital with my little guy.

My days consisted of waking up to a host of drugs and needle pricks, followed, like clockwork, by the footsteps of my three year old who came to the hospital first thing in the morning, every morning. He was brought to the hospital every day by either my husband (if my mom spent the night at the hospital with me) or by my mom (when my husband spent the night with me).

I was blessed to have either of them there every single day that I was there, and I was especially blessed to have my full-of-energy three year old turn the corner and exclaim, "Hi mommy. I'm here!" and spend the whole day with me until it was time to go home. He was a true delight to me, and to all the nurses and doctors he met during those visits.

The hardest day ever was when my blood pressure was finally low enough for me to be released from the hospital. On that day I got sent home without my baby boy. It didn't hit home that I would have to leave him there until I was rolled into the lobby, and as I looked around for my son, I realized that he was still upstairs in the NICU and that I would have to leave him there. I (understandably) lost it, and I cried until I ran out of tears, but within a few hours, despite warnings to "take it easy" since I'd had a C-section, I was back to visit my son.

There were many things that could have, and should have, gone wrong but did not. When my son was born, at only 1 pound, 11.7 ounces, I was told that I would not get to hold him for a week. He was so small it was certainly understandable. I consoled myself with the fact that at least my husband had held him on the day he was born, albeit briefly. But it was still heartbreaking to look at our little guy and not be able to hold him and kiss his toes or rub his head.

The first day I went in to see him, the day after I'd had him, I was so sick that I threw up in the room, right next to his incubator. I was embarrassed, and devastated, and thought that at that rate I would never get to hold him. But at least I'd get to see him.

And see him I did. I visited my little guy every day, five or more times per day, to the point where the nurses started to warn me that if I didn't rest more I would get sick and wouldn't be able to visit him at all. Following that warning I scaled back my visits to three per day.

On the fourth day of my little guy's birth, I went to see him and was told by his nurse, Marianne, that I could hold him. Tears immediately fell from my eyes as I held my little guy, so small, in my arms. From that day forward I was able to hold him every day. From holding him I was able to move to changing him, checking his temperature, doing his daily care. From there I was able to have skin to skin contact with him, then breastfeed him.

Even though we had been warned of all that could go wrong, nothing did. My son gained weight steadily, and was soon considered a feeder-grower (meaning he was in the NICU not because he was sick but because he needed to get big enough to go home). We were told that our son wasn't even considered intensive care (despite the name: neonatal intensive care unit). He was considered intermediate care.

Our testimony became even stronger as our son got bigger and older in the NICU. We talked and prayed to God steadily throughout his course in the NICU. Every day we visited, at every single visit, we would stand over his incubator, and later his crib when he was moved out of the incubator, and we would pray. We asked God to post his angels before, behind, on either side, above and below our son's incubator, then crib, and watch over him all night long. We asked God to bless our son with grace, mercy and favor, and indeed He did.

The doctors often came into our room to express bewilderment at how well our little guy was doing in the NICU, and how remarkably smooth his course in the NICU had been.

At some point, during a conversation with God, he revealed to me that our son would be coming home at 36 weeks gestation[6]. That was to be a full month before he would have even been born, or even due for that matter. I got this confirmation when our little guy had only been in the NICU for

---

[6] Gestation refers to the period of time from conception to birth. When I say "36 weeks gestation" this is how far along I would have been if I'd still been pregnant. Even though I was no longer pregnant, this is how preemie babies' ages are calculated in the NICU.

about three weeks (at that point he was only 30 weeks gestation).

Needless to say, at that early time there was no way to know when he would be released. On an almost daily basis the nurses would "warn"[7] us that our son would likely be in the NICU well past his due date, not because he was sick or had any issues, but because he had been so small at birth. I would tell them, "No, he's coming home at 36 weeks." The nurses would gently warn me not to get my hopes up. They would remind me that things could change and take a turn for the worse.

Even though there were times their warnings were annoying and seemingly pessimistic, I knew they came from an experienced place. Because the NICU nurses had been in these situations and had seen so many things (complications, adverse outcomes) and because they knew that, statistically, my baby was supposed to have issues (based on his weight

---

[7] The nurses were wonderful and did not give us those warnings (that our son would more than likely be in the NICU past his due date) because they were trying to be mean. Quite the contrary, the nurses sought to prepare us, so that we wouldn't get fixated on a hospital release date for our little guy and become brokenhearted if that date came and went. The NICU nurses at Virtua Hospital in Voorhees, New Jersey are a group of wonderful, patient, loving women and men. They are true blessings!

and based on the issues other babies his gestational age and weight had) they were just telling me what they knew to be true. They were basing their expectations of their training and experience.

But how many of us know that God has the final answer? That He's best at showing what He's capable of during times when we (with our degrees, and our education, and our money, and our "stuff") can go no further? It is during such times that we can truly see that He can do the impossible, that He can do ALL things, and that nothing is too hard for God!

And boy, oh boy, did He do the impossible for us!

He blessed us to get to the hospital to investigate my "stomachache" just in time to be diagnosed with severe preeclampsia, HELLP Syndrome. I later learned that as many as 6 out of 10 babies can die from a mother afflicted with HELLP Syndrome[8]. I thank God that I did not come across that statistic while in the hospital.

The doctors said that if we had waited any longer to come in, that my condition would have worsened and I could have lost my life and that of

[8] American Pregnancy Association

my unborn child. The doctors also told us that what caused us to come in (the nausea/constipation feeling) was usually not a presenting symptom, but I believe God used that to get us into that hospital. How else would we have known that the "knot at the top of my stomach" was actually my swollen liver!

And still, the blessings continued.

We were blessed to have a successful, uncomplicated, emergency C-section. He then blessed us with our son. We could really feel the prayers of our families, as God's grace was bestowed upon our son from the time he came out three months early, weighing 1 lb., 11.7 oz., to the time he came home at 36 weeks gestation, 4 weeks before he was even due to be born!

God had even revealed to me his intention to release my son from the NICU and the hospital one month early, thus revealing His awesome power and omniscience. When I told my husband, family, and the nurses that my little guy would come home at 36 weeks, he was only 2 lbs. and there was no way I could've or should've known when he would be released from the hospital.

But that's the goodness of God. He made it so that my son's journey would prove everyone wrong, and defy conventional and "professional" wisdom, so we would truly know that this blessing (or miracle as it was referred to in the hospital) was from Him.

My son is now 8 months old[9]. He is huge, weighing in at over the 100th percentile (which means that he is bigger than over 100% of babies his age). He is strong and still has that feisty personality that he had at birth. He is the happiest, silliest baby ever, and is our true blessing from God (along with his big brother). This book is dedicated to him, as I made a promise to God that I would make sure that his story was told. I promised that I would make his story a testimony, a demonstration of God's love, power, and grace.

---

[9] He is now over a year old and is still huge!

Testimony 3: God Offers Protection from Hurt, Harm, and Danger

I did not want to go in to work that day. You hear that all the time with these kinds of stories, but it's true.

From the moment I woke up, I did not want to go. What made me go was the fact that my calling off would have been last minute and would have inconvenienced other people, and I did not want to call off and leave my boss stranded, unable to find someone to work my shift. Especially on a Saturday.

Saturdays at hotels were usually pretty busy, so I didn't want to shrug-off my responsibility onto someone else. With resolve, I determined that I would go in to work.

My shift started at 3 p.m. Before that, however, I had some shopping to do! I was shopping with my mom for a new computer. The computer was my college graduation gift from my mom. We went to a computer store, and after looking at every computer that was there, I finally settled on the perfect one!

This was such an exciting time for me. I was excited to own my own computer, I was excited that I would be going away to graduate school in pursuit of a Ph.D., and I was excited to be moving into an apartment. There were so many great things happening in my life at that time. I truly couldn't ask for more.

I was having so much fun with my mom, shopping for a computer, that I didn't notice the time. By the time we had checked out, it was 2:30 p.m. I had 30 minutes to get to work, and I desperately didn't want to go.

Of the $1,000 I had been given towards my computer, I still had about $200 leftover, so I wanted to shop some more. I wanted to go to lunch with my mom and talk about how great it would be to be living in my own apartment (by the grace of God I had been given a three- bedroom apartment for the price of a one-bedroom. The realtor said I'd gotten lucky and was given that deal because a three-bedroom apartment was all that was left, whereas the one-bedrooms had sold out. But I knew that it was a blessing from God), and now I wanted to shop some more and buy some nice things for the new, spacious apartment I would be moving into when school started.

I wanted to go see a movie, I thought about going to see a friend, about hanging out at my grandmother's house and just chatting it up.

I thought of everything I could be doing except working.

I was on such a shopping buzz and the last thing I wanted to do was end it by going to work. My shift was from 3-11 p.m. Coming from such an exciting day I knew those would be some of the longest hours of my life. And boy was I right. I had no idea how right I was about the long day I was about to have.

Still, I went in to work. We loaded my new computer into the back of my mom's truck so she could get it home safely, and I tucked the $200 down into the bottom of my purse. I pulled out a $5.00 bill and put it on top. The $5.00 would be for lunch while at work.

When I got to work it was 3 p.m. on the dot. I relieved the person who had worked the morning shift (7 a.m. to 3 p.m.) and set about my duties.

I had been working as a hotel front desk clerk for two years and I loved the job. It allowed me to do my class work when the hotel wasn't busy, and because there were so few employees, I could always pick up extra shifts. It was not uncommon for me to work 50 or more hours per week while going to school full time. As a matter of fact, I got more class work done while at work than at home.

When I first started my shift, some of my duties included checking the computer for incoming reservations, checking to make sure we had fresh towels, and counting the cash drawer.

When I had done those duties and a few others, I sat in the chair behind the desk and started to read a newspaper.

At some point it got a little chilly behind the desk, so I put on the jacket I usually packed to bring to work. On that particular day I was not wearing my work shirt, but was wearing a cute little summer top that showed a bit of cleavage at the top. Not a lot – and I didn't know it at the time - but having that jacket on and zipped all the way to the neck, with my cleavage covered would become a potential blessing in disguise.

About an hour after I had been at work, I noticed a person on the outside camera walking toward the front office where I was. As a general rule, I always kept the office doors locked until I saw a customer approach. I don't really know why I used to do this. I guess it made me feel safer.

The hotel where I worked was a bit secluded. It was off the highway - with the highway to the right and a neighborhood to the left. It also shared the same parking lot with another hotel. The other hotel was also owned by the same people, and it sat out front, while the hotel I worked at was housed behind it.

People were always walking through the parking lot, either as a shortcut to get to the bordering neighborhood or just because, so I never really felt unsafe. Still, I used to lock those doors.

Since I saw someone approaching, I stood up and looked through the window for a better view. It was the other front desk clerk from the hotel in front of my own and she was walking very close with a young man. I unsnapped the lock that was located under the desk to let her (and who I assumed was her boyfriend) in, then I stood behind the counter to wait for them to approach the desk.

My coworker was indeed one of the people who approached the desk, but the other person was not her boyfriend. The other person was a masked man holding a gun to the back of her head and talking to me.

I stood there in stunned silence. Seeing it all, but as if not really being there. I saw her standing there with a look of terror on her face, and I saw him pointing the gun at her, then at me. After what seemed like an eternity I heard him say something to me then point the gun at me.

He was standing on the other side of the counter, she was standing beside him, and he was pointing the gun at my forehead and telling me to lock the door back. I did as he said, and he came around the counter with my coworker in tow and stood right beside me. He then yelled at me to give him all the money in the cash register.

I opened the cash register and started taking out the money, my hands were shaking, and I guess I wasn't moving fast enough because he then placed the gun at the back of my head[10] and said, "Bitch, hurry up!" I know it doesn't make sense, but I remember wondering why he had called me a bitch.

---

[10] For years after this happened I would randomly feel that gun pressed against the back of my head. It took years before the image and the feeling of that cold metal against the back of my head went away.

When I had loaded the money in the bag, all while he kept the gun firmly pressed against the back of my head, he moved us over to the safe. I don't know how he knew there was a safe in the first place. Maybe he had just seen it as he stood behind me while I collected the money from the cash register for him. Or maybe he'd already planned to try to get it.

Whatever the case, he made my coworker and I try to unlock it. And when we nervously tried to explain that we didn't have the key, he put the gun to my head again and said, "Bitch, stop playing with me." I said, "I swear to God we don't have it!" Again, I wondered why I'd said that. I never say "I swear to God." That was not something I had ever said before, but I said it then and he dropped the gun from my head.

He then made us try to figure out what the combination was. When that attempt failed, he grew even more frustrated with us and walked over to my purse, which was sitting next to the desk where I had been sitting just minutes before. He told me "Give me all your money." I said, "I don't have any." And before he could raise that gun again, I said "You can check if you want."

Again, that was unusual. I did, in fact, have money. I had $200, and for the life of me I do not know why I kept that from that robber. I knew then and I know now that $200 is not worth my life. And I realize that I should have willingly handed it over, but I didn't. And I don't know why. It's almost like someone else was speaking for me, guiding me along that terrible ordeal.

After I told him I didn't have any money, he walked us back around the counter. He then told me to go back to where we had come from and grab a room key. I grabbed one, not stopping to think for a second what he wanted with it. He walked us into the hallway and towards the rooms, and that's when I panicked and started to wonder what he was going to do to us.

If he brought us to one of the rooms he could've raped and/or killed us and no one would have known unless they had specifically checked those rooms. And that probably wouldn't have happened until the next morning when housekeeping showed up to clean the rooms. Even then, there were many rooms, so finding us that next day was no guarantee.

We started to walk with him toward the rooms with my mind racing, when all of a sudden he turned around toward the stairs leading to the second floor and told us to run. It happened so quickly. He changed his mind and told us to run so suddenly that my first thought was that he was going to shoot us in the back.

My coworker must have been thinking the same thing because both she and I hesitantly began to walk away from him and towards the stairs. I guess we weren't moving fast enough because the robber then shouted, "I said, RUN!" And we did. We ran as fast and as far as our legs could carry us. We ran up the stairs and away from the robber before he could shoot us and before he re-changed his mind and took us into one of those rooms to do God only knows what to us.

After we had run across the second floor of the hotel, we ran down the second flight of stairs, scared that he was still on the first floor waiting to kill us. We ran fast and slow all at the same time (if that's even possible). On the one hand we were trying to get away and on the other hand we wanted to make sure we gave him enough time to leave so we wouldn't run into him again.

When we ran past the office we saw that it was empty, so we ran inside and locked ourselves in there, and that's when we called the police.

That's also when I lost it.

By the grace of God I had managed to keep it together while the armed robber was there, but when the reality set in, and my mind processed what had just happened and what could have happened, my body began to shake and convulse so hard that I could not stand. I had to sit on the floor and hold myself in a tight ball.

Just a few minutes later, as we were waiting for the police to arrive, my older brother arrived. He was driving by and had decided to check in on me, and I don't believe it was a coincidence, I believe God sent him.

The police arrived and I was shaking so uncontrollably that I had to sit on the police car. I could not stand. My older brother had stopped by my job to check on me and proved to be a great comfort and sense of support as I sat there in his arms, convulsing uncontrollably, and telling the police what had happened.

I later found out that the situation was both much worse and much better than I had known.

The situation was much worse than I knew in that I found out later that day that in addition to the

armed robber robbing the first hotel that day
(before he walked my coworker over to me), but
he had also sexually assaulted her. He had walked
her over to the hotel to rob me, after putting her
through a far worse ordeal than what I had gone
through.

I thought back to what I had been wearing just
minutes before the robber came. I wondered if
God had me cover up in that jacket so that I would
not give the robber any sexual ideas and invite
further harm onto myself. I realized that that could
have happened to me. I realized that that guy could
have just as easily robbed my hotel first, thus
inflicting that additional trauma onto me.

My heart hurt for the young lady that had to go
through that. Yet, ashamed for thinking it, I was
also grateful that God had shielded me from that.

The situation was much better, indeed a blessing,
in that despite being shaken up during the whole
ordeal, I had wanted to tell the armed robber that I
knew he wouldn't hurt me.

Even as I write this I am trying to figure out the
best words to use to express what I felt during the
robbery. It was like I was encased in a bubble.
Although I knew, technically, that I was in harm's

way, I also knew something that even the robber didn't know. I knew that he was not going to hurt me. I knew that he wouldn't be allowed.

And this is strange for a number of reasons. One of which is because I remember wondering to myself how many people had survived a gunshot wound to the head (when that robber put that gun to my head the second time). So even as I was trying to encourage myself that others had survived a gunshot wound to the head and that I could possibly survive it too - which means I must have been preparing myself to be shot - I was also feeling enclosed in a bubble like the guy wouldn't, couldn't hurt me.

I have shed so many tears after this trauma. But, surprisingly, I only cry when I am trying to explain that feeling of protection I felt. That feeling of being wrapped in a bubble that was so strong, so tangible, that I even wanted to share the news of it with the robber!

To this day, eight years after being robbed at gunpoint, trying to verbalize that feeling still moves me to tears. And I am no crier. The feeling was simply magical. Supernatural.

The next day at church, before the sermon even began, I burst into tears. I was overwhelmed by the goodness of God. I imagine the devil expected me to renounce God. To question Him. To doubt Him. But what I did instead was thank Him. I had never felt so protected in the midst of something so scary before.

I remembered how I'd felt encased, enclosed, protected. I remembered how that armed robber had changed his mind and instead of taking us into one of those rooms had told us to run. It had happened so suddenly that I think it even shocked the robber. I don't think he intended to say those words. I firmly believe that God's grace and mercy flowed through that troubled young man and freed us from whatever evil he had intended for us.

I remembered how God sent my brother to my job to check on me, to hold and comfort me as I responded to what had happened. I was never more in love with God than in that moment. And my heart filled with gratitude that not even 24 hours prior, I had been staring down the barrel of a gun and had lived to talk about it. I loved Him so much! And the only way I could express it was through tears.

I believe God saw my heart that day and He understood my praise as I cried all the way through church that Sunday morning.

Update: That armed robber was never caught. I pray that wherever he is, he has given his life to God.

Testimony 4: God Uses Everything for the Benefit of Those Who Love Him

It had been a whirlwind year, and we were only halfway through it! I had graduated from college with honors, had been accepted into a Ph.D. program, had been awarded a fellowship that would pay my full tuition, had been blessed with a three-bedroom apartment for the price of a one-bedroom, and an out-of-the-blue check for over $4,000[11].

It hadn't all been roses, however, because I had also been robbed at gunpoint in broad daylight while on my job. But even then I had felt totally protected. Even in the midst of danger, I had felt God's peace and had been ensconced in His loving arms. I knew full well that the situation could have been much worse than it was, and for at least one other person it had been, but God had covered me.

In my whirlwind year of blessings on top of blessings on top of blessings, and even a traumatic event, I had truly experienced God's favor, His grace, and His mercy.

---

[11] See Testimony #6.

I prided myself on the fact that I had praised Him through it all. I knew that it was easy to praise Him when things were going well, but I had praised Him just as much when I had received that $4,000 check as when I was robbed at gunpoint. Throughout the highest highs and the lowest lows I had given Him the glory. I was proud of that. Although to a far lesser extent, it made me think I had passed my Job[12] test (pronounced Joeb, rhymes with robe).

I had not gone back to that job after being robbed at gunpoint. I was an adult, but my parents and brothers had absolutely forbidden it. The thought of me going back to the job had my family in such an uproar, that I couldn't have gone back even if I'd wanted to. Still, I had a lot of things to buy to get ready for my move to a new state and a new apartment to start graduate school. But it seems that God had thought of everything. Because of the $4,000 check, I had been able to get the furniture I needed, as well as any other incidentals.

One of those incidentals was a car. Although I'd already had a car for college (a 1989 Toyota Camry with a leaky sunroof) my dad wanted me to get

---

[12] Job is a book in the bible detailing the struggle of Job, a man of God who was tested with a series of trials and losses, but who never gave up on God.

something more reliable for those drives back home as well as around the town where my school was located. The last thing he wanted, he'd said, was for me to find myself stranded in a city where I didn't know anyone and was so far from home. I agreed, and off we went shopping for a used car.

Just to be clear, my dad's and my idea of what a "good" car is differs...drastically. My dad values reliability above looks, and I valued looks as much as reliability. It seems the more reliable the car was, the uglier it was. My dad seemed to be drawn to the ugliest cars he could find. And whenever I found something even remotely sporty-looking, my dad gave me 10 reasons why it would break down on me. We were like our own little sitcom. Let's just say those were an interesting few weeks.

My dad finally wore me down and we reached a "compromise". Instead of the two-door little navy blue car that I wanted, my dad insisted that the Ford Taurus would be more reliable. My price range was limited, obviously, and for the money he said I would get a lot of value. So even though there was nothing even remotely sporty about this Taurus, it at least had a pretty silver color, and my dad assured me that I could always get tint added if I wanted. And yes, I definitely wanted.

So we bought the Taurus. It was a 1997 Ford Taurus. Nothing flashy, but reliable. As foretold by my dad, it checked out when we had it independently inspected, and as if on cue, the 1997 navy blue two-door Saturn that I'd had my eyes on and that had been driven off the lot by another customer (making my dad happy and me sad) had been returned on the same day because it had started smoking and making funny noises. My dad didn't bother telling me "I told you so." But he did give me a "look". Ok. So he was right.

Anyway, I bought the Taurus using some of the cash that I had as well as the trade-in of my old Toyota Camry and off I went. The car, I must admit, drove great. It was comfy, the AC was great, and just to satisfy my urges for a sporty car I'd had it tinted and had a 10-disc CD changer installed in the trunk. The car was reliable and now semi-sporty - best of both worlds.

One day I awoke early and went outside to retrieve something out of my glove compartment. I saw my grandmother's car, and I saw that two of the other cars were missing. My mom's car was missing because she was at work, but why was my car missing?

It took me a moment to realize that my car had been stolen!

The spot where my car had been parked was now a big empty space with nothing there other than some of the mail and papers I'd had in my glove compartment. I walked around the empty space in pure shock. I guess I was trying to make sure the car was really gone, and that I wasn't dreaming. It was equivalent to "pinching myself".

When it set in that my car had indeed been stolen, I ran inside and screamed for my family to wake up. My older brother, younger brother, and my grandmother were all at my mom's house at that time, and they all began to slowly wake up and groggily respond to my news.

When it finally registered, they sprang into action and we called the police. When the police got there we filed a report and gave them all the information they needed. Then we went driving around in hopes of finding my stolen car.

I was angry! So very angry! I can rarely remember being that angry, not before or after that day. And it wasn't about the car. I had never been "in love" with that car. No offense, but it was a Ford Taurus, purchased to get me from one place to the next. It wasn't my dream car or anything, and it hadn't cost a ridiculous amount of money. So it wasn't about the car. It was about what had happened before the car was stolen.

Just six short weeks before, I had been robbed at gunpoint. In broad daylight, while at my job. Before that I had never experienced crime or violence. We had been raised right. As Christians, we were taught to pray and trust in God. To live lives that would glorify God. We had been in Catholic School all our lives. We prayed before school started, during school, before lunch, after recess, before school let out. We weren't living lives of crime, nor were we allowed to associate with people who did.

That day when I was robbed, I had been at work, earning a living. Not that it would have been justified, but I had not been at the club, out partying, drinking, or smoking. I had been at work. On a Saturday. Three o'clock in the afternoon.

During the robbery, that gun had been placed at the back of my head two times. I could still feel the metal of the gun at the back of my head. I would feel it when I woke in the morning, as I drove places, in the shower, during dinner. It would come on whenever, wherever and would leave me feeling sad, angry, and shaken.

I had no control over when it came, and I resented the way it made me feel. But I praised God even in the midst of it. I thanked Him every time I felt that metal, every time I recalled that afternoon. Every time I watched the news and another young person had been murdered, senselessly. I knew it could have been me. And I praised God. I had been robbed at gunpoint and instead of it shaking my faith, it had strengthened it.

But now I was mad. Hadn't I gone through enough? Hadn't I proved myself? Hadn't I passed the test? So why was I experiencing trauma again? Why was I being victimized again? And so soon after the first ordeal? I didn't think it was right. I didn't think it was fair. And despite going through the first ordeal without questioning God, this time I wanted answers.

While driving around in my grandmother's Impala with my big brother driving, my grandmother in the front seat, and myself and my little brother in the backseat, with Smokie Norful playing on the car's stereo, I asked God if He was real. I asked Him what the point of being a Christian was if I couldn't expect to be saved from hurt, harm, or danger. I asked Him if He'd really saved me last time, or if it was by chance that I didn't get killed that day as I was being robbed. I asked Him if I had just imagined that whole "bubble of protection".

I got deep. I went even further and asked Him why children were killed, and why women were raped, and men gunned down like dogs in the street, if He was real. I sat in the back of that car, angry, growing more annoyed as I listened to Smokie Norful sing about God (no doubt my grandmother's silent way of encouraging and consoling me).

I asked God about school. Flippantly, I asked God if He had bothered to consider how I was going to get to school, out of state, if I didn't have a car. School was starting in less than a month. I wondered if He cared that I wouldn't be able to go, since I didn't have a car, and couldn't live out of state without transportation. I wondered if He cared that I would have to decline my acceptance into the program, give up the scholarship that would pay my tuition, lose out on my hopes and dreams of becoming a Psychologist because I wouldn't be able to attend school.

I reasoned that He didn't care at all since He had let this happen. I questioned His "all-powerful" persona. I wondered what kind of "power" couldn't stop a petty car thief.

I cringe when I write this. I cringe at the disrespect I showed to my Lord and Saviour. I cringe when in those moments I was able to forget about how He had delivered me from the enemy and saved my life as I was being robbed.

I cringe when I forget about the blessings he'd bestowed upon me just months before, in ways I wouldn't have been able to attribute to anyone or anything else.

Isn't it funny how we question Him when the going gets tough? How flimsy our faith is? How easily we forget all the good He's done in our lives when we experience something adversarial?

I thought I had passed my Job test, but unlike Job who passed, for me, when the going got tough and then tougher still, I failed - miserably. I was ready to renounce my Lord and Saviour behind a stolen car that I didn't like all that much in the first place.

Well, luckily for me God uses every situation to improve us. Even when we fail miserably like I did then, and have since, and will again, He never leaves or forsakes us. Not even when we so clearly forsake Him.

We found my car that night.

After driving around for about nine hours, stopping only to grab fast-food and use the restroom, we found my car rammed up against a brick building a block from the housing projects. The housing projects were home to some of the city's poorest citizens. And there sat my car, wrecked, kicked, trashed.

The car thieves, no doubt youths, had left sunflower seeds all over my car. I guess that had been their joyriding snack. Oddly enough, they had also been listening to a tape of one of my pastor's church sermons while riding around in my car that they had stolen.

I used to purchase cassettes of all the sermons, or at least of the ones that had particularly moved me, and would keep them in the car so that I could hear them as I drove. The car thieves had listened to one of those cassettes. They had popped that cassette into my car's tape deck and had listened to the tape in its entirety. They even went so far as to turn the tape around to hear the other side.

Ah ha, I thought. Was that the point? Were they supposed to hear a word from God? Did God use this "opportunity" to plant a word in the lives of the young people that had stolen my car? Did He know that that was the only way to get to them?

Or even if it wasn't the only way, was it the way He wanted to use? Was what was on that tape necessary for one or more of the young people in that car to hear? Did it lead to their salvation? Did they get out of my car because they had been convicted (by God), and were ashamed of what they'd done? Did the next Sunday find them in church? After all this, did they give their lives to Christ?

I learned a few valuable lessons that day. One, I had a lot of growing to do spiritually. I realized my faith was weak, and I had to work to strengthen it. I asked God for His forgiveness for doubting Him, and I asked to be put back in His good graces. Then I rested comfortably knowing that it was done.

The wonderful thing about God is that He never leaves us, even when we leave Him. He is there, waiting to be invited back into our lives - anytime, anywhere, no matter what we've done. That gives me chills.

Second, I learned that when we say The Lord's Prayer[13] or any other prayer that asks for His will to be done, we are submitting to Him, and He will use

---

[13] "The Lord's Prayer" is also known as "The Our Father Prayer". To read it in full, with various translations, see the Postface at the end of this book.

that. He will use us. If we allow Him, if we ask Him, He will use us. So don't ask if you don't mean it. And don't submit if you are not ready for what comes with that submission.

The reassuring thing is that He provides for us even as He uses us. He clears a path and makes a way and "pays us back" for our services. It has been my experience that whenever He uses me, He makes it completely worth my while.

For example, God used my car to deliver His word to those troubled youth. But He did not leave me stranded. Although my car was not drivable, having been too badly damaged, and needing almost a complete rebuild (it was deemed a total lost but I chose to get it repaired anyway because I needed a vehicle), a couple weeks after my car was broken into and while it was being repaired, my grandmother broke her wrist, rendering her incapable of driving for two months, so she gave me her car to go to school in.

Now, my God didn't break my grandmother's wrist. And I don't think He allowed it to happen just for me to have a car to drive in. But I think He uses everything – EVERYTHING- for the benefit of those who love Him and are called according to His will. He used that situation to provide me with the transportation I needed to get to school. And wouldn't you know it that it took my grandmother two months to completely heal, and it also took the same two months for my car to be repaired and returned to me?

It worked out such that the same weekend that I drove back home to pick up my car was the weekend that my grandmother's doctor cleared her for driving again. What do you think about that? Amazing, right? That's just the kind of God we serve.

Testimony 5[14]: God Walks With Us…Literally

"A young university student was home for the summer. She had gone to visit some friends one evening and time passed quickly as each shared their various experiences of the past year. She ended up staying longer than planned, and had to walk home alone. She wasn't afraid because it was a small town and she lived only a few blocks away.

As she walked along under the tall elm trees, she asked God to keep her safe from harm and danger. When she reached the alley, which was a shortcut to her house, she decided to take it. However, halfway down the alley she noticed a man standing at the end as though he was waiting for her.

She became uneasy and began to pray, asking for God's protection. Instantly a comforting feeling of

---

[14] This story was sent to me by one of those mass emails many years ago. By "mass emails" I am referring to the kind of emails that have thousands of recipients and just as many senders because everyone keeps adding additional recipients and then forwarding it along. The thing is, it came at a time when I needed it most. I printed it out, hung it up in my office, and have kept it nearby ever since. I am sharing it in this book because it is a great and powerful illustration of God's power, His love, and the power of prayer. I am attaching it nearly verbatim to the email I received so long ago. May its original sender be blessed.

quietness and security wrapped around her, she felt as though someone was walking with her. When she reached the end of the alley, she walked right past the man and arrived home safely.

The following day, she read in the newspaper that a young girl had been raped in the same alley just twenty minutes after she had been there. Feeling overwhelmed by this tragedy and the fact that it could have been her, she began to weep. Thanking the Lord for her safety and to help this young woman, she decided to go to the police station. She felt she could recognize the man, so she told them her story.

The police asked her if she would be willing to look at a lineup to see if she could identify him. She agreed and immediately pointed out the man she had seen in the alley the night before.

When the man was told he had been identified, he immediately broke down and confessed. The officer thanked the young woman for her bravery and asked if there was anything they could do for her. She asked if they would ask the man one question. The young woman was curious as to why he had not attacked her. When the policeman asked him, he answered, 'Because she wasn't alone. She had two tall men walking on either side of her.'"

Angels exist and prayer works. Try it.

Testimony 6: God Provides Increase, Overflow, and Favor

I had been going to church all my life. But it was more of a formality. It wasn't personal. It was expected of me. At the age of nine I was baptized, and the most exciting part about getting baptized was getting "dipped" in the water and wearing the beautiful white gown.

Getting baptized was just another expectation. It held no meaning other than pleasing my mom.

Admittedly, to me, the best part of church was the donuts before and after Sunday School. I would count down the time to when the preacher would (finally) wrap it up, or I'd try to fall asleep without my mom noticing and popping me in the back of the head.

When I was 14 my mom started going to a new church. Our previous church had been the family church. It was where my parents were married and where my mom had grown up, and maybe even where her parents were married.

But when we moved to a different part of town, because my parents had split up, we started attending a new church. I rebelled at the idea. I didn't want to move to a new house, and I certainly didn't want to go to a new church (they were all equally boring as far as I was concerned).

In addition to my rebellion about changing what I had always known and done was the fact that I had already heard some things about this church. It was one of those mega churches with several locations and several sermons. Even in my 14-year-old mind it seemed to be more about making money than about "serving God", so I was plenty skeptical.

I attended the service arms folded, lips pouting, head cocked to the side. While my mom ignored me and sang along, I sneered at the elaborate setting of the church. I rolled my eyes when all of the ladies stood, dressed as if they were going to prom. I laughed inwardly (because I didn't want to get in trouble) whenever I heard a blunder. And I just basically planned to bide my time until church was over and we went out to eat. We always went out to eat after church, and I secretly entertained myself by thinking of what I planned to order.

Finally the sermon started. The pastor walked out in his fancy purple robe (did he think he was royalty?) and began to preach. Despite my resistance, and I assure you I was putting up a good fight, the message got to me and I found myself enjoying the sermon. When church was over, I was actually sad. I wanted more. Even today I can still vividly remember that sermon.

Not easily dismayed (I was, after all, 14 and thought I knew everything), I decided that that particular sermon was a fluke and that the next one would expose this church for the fraud that it was. However, just like the week before, at the next sermon the following week I was moved again. And this time I was moved to tears. I am not a "crier", and my mom knew this, so even she was shocked to see me so emotional. By the next Sunday I had joined the church. I had found a spiritual home.

This church was different from anything I had ever experienced. I found it exciting. It taught me things and made me realize that even at my age I could live a life that was pleasing to God.

This in itself was shocking, as despite growing up in the church and around very spiritual women, I had never been a God-fanatic. I thought He was cool, and I believed in Him (because I had been told to and I was afraid not to), but I'd never really heard from Him or had a personal relationship with Him. Then all of a sudden it began to build.

I found myself talking to my friends about God, and about doing the right things. I stopped using profanity at school. Although my parents never knew I used profanity, because "cursing" wasn't allowed in our home, I had picked up a few things from TV and from my friends, and we used to walk around the playground cursing, just because we wanted to.

Well, I stopped. I started trying to talk my friends out of rolling up their skirts to make them seem shorter and more appealing to the boys. Although that wasn't something I did (courtesy of the fact that my dad was a supervisor at his job and could drive up to my school at any moment and catch me). I talked to them about not letting the boys kiss them or peek under their skirts (again, not something I did because I was afraid of my dad and because my big brother also attended the same school as me and could've found out). I became so "righteous" that the boys in my class started calling me a "dyke[15]" and saying I didn't like boys, I only liked girls.

---

[15] The term "Dyke" was a derogatory, slang term that was used back in the day to refer to a lesbian, or a woman who dated or was attracted to other women.

Still, I resisted temptation and stood up for what I believed. I was (and still am) a leader, so I wasn't easily deterred. I'm also not overly sensitive (remember I said I'm not a crier) so I wasn't easily offended.

I was, and am, far from perfect. To this day I have a fiery temper and managed to graduate from elementary school as the Valedictorian but on probation for fighting. But that's another story and another testimony for another day. The point is, I continued to practice and grow in my faith, developing and strengthening along the way.

On one particular Sunday the pastor preached about tithing. He told us that everything belonged to God and that God was trusting us and testing our faith to see if we would give Him back 10% of what He'd given us in the first place.

The pastor said it wasn't about the money, because God could get anything from anywhere if He wanted it. But that it was more about our obedience. And whether or not we were willing to submit to God's will.

The pastor told us that we would be rewarded for our obedience, and that any tithes we paid would be "paid back" to us, sometimes 30%, sometimes

60%, and other times 100% fold. He reiterated that tithing was not about being paid back, because not every gift would be monetary, but that it was about obedience, and doing what God tells us to do - which includes tithing.

The pastor had the tithers of the church hold up their tithing envelopes and ask The Lord for "Increase, Overflow, and Favor". I took that message to heart, and carried it with me. I still do.

As time went on I got my first job and started to tithe. I was working at Wendy's after school and obviously didn't make a lot of money. But I faithfully gave my 10%. I gave it joyfully, even when it meant I didn't have enough left over to get that pair of boots, or my hair done, or whatever I fancied as a teenager.

When I finished high school and went to college, I moved up in position from a fast food worker to a front desk clerk at a hotel. I worked full time at the hotel and went to school full time.

At first I continued to tithe 10%. But eventually I began to tithe 15%. I felt I wanted to give God extra. Although no major blessing (that I knew of) had happened to me to "warrant" the extra money, I just really wanted to give God more than what He asked because He had already done enough in my life.

I continued to go to church, read my bible, and tithe. And every time I tithed I raised my envelope and asked God for "Increase, Overflow, and Favor".

Before I knew it, I was a senior in college and it was time to get ready to apply for graduate school. I had wanted to be a Psychologist to help others, so I knew I would have to get a Ph.D. That was the only way to become a Psychologist. So I started to prepare.

I already had good grades in college, and was well on my way to graduating with honors. I had also completed a year and a half long research study, thus proving my ability to conduct research, which is what a Ph.D. is all about. The next step was to find a Ph.D. program that had professors with similar research interests as mine.

I looked around, and came across the school I wanted. As I researched further I found that this particular school required that students get a Master's degree first, then wait one year before pursuing the doctorate, which I did not want to do. Patience has never been my virtue, and since I already knew that the doctorate (Ph.D.) would take many years to complete, I certainly didn't want to prolong the process by waiting around for a year before I could finish up.

I kindly thanked the program director for the information. And when she asked me if I was still interested in the program so she could send me an admission packet, I told her, honestly, that I was no longer interested. I told her that I wanted a program that would allow me to go straight through without waiting the year between degrees.

The program director very kindly recommended a school I had not heard of before. She said that particular school didn't have that one year waiting requirement. I thanked her and immediately looked up the other school. Although I had never heard of them, they were a big school. Their Ph.D. program was fully accredited and there was a professor in the department with similar research interests.

I was so excited! I called up the program director, and was dismayed to find that the deadline to apply was in two days. I hurriedly sent in all my transcripts, wrote the proper letters of interest, and requested letters of recommendation from my own professors. I over-nighted the whole package, with the exception of the GRE[16] scores.

The GRE is required to get into graduate school, but two days wouldn't be enough time to take the test. So, what I did instead was register for the next available test (which was a few weeks away) and I submitted proof of my GRE registration along with a carefully written note that assured the program coordinator and director that even though I had not yet taken the GRE, that I was a great test-taker (very true) and that I had no doubt whatsoever that I would meet the test's minimum acceptance requirements.

I assured them that I would score off the charts on the test and that it would be no problem. I then over-nighted my packet and waited to hear back.

Three weeks later, when it was time to take the GRE, I was nervous. It was true that I had always been a great test-taker. When I took the entrance test to get into a Catholic, all-girls high school, I scored so well that in addition to inviting me to attend the school, they offered me a scholarship. We didn't even know that you could win a

---

[16] The GRE (Graduate Records Examination) is a standardized examination that measures verbal and quantitative skills.

scholarship to a high school, or even that there was a scholarship to win!

Also, when the ACT[17] came around, I scored so high that the school principal made an announcement at the school's assembly! That was how I found out that the ACT scores were even back! I also received so many college interest letters and scholarship offers that I could have truly attended anywhere I wanted.

So, needless to say, I shouldn't have been nervous. But I was. And that was a new feeling. I tried to reason that my nervousness was because so much was on the line, for example, getting accepted into a Ph.D. program and realizing my dream of becoming a Psychologist. Or maybe the nervousness was because I'd only had a few weeks to prepare for the GRE, since I'd had to register really quickly so I could apply to the program. Whatever the case, I was nervous, but not worried. I knew I would test well. I always did.

Well, things didn't go as planned. The good thing about the GRE is that you find out your scores immediately. Just as soon as you've completed the

---

[17] The ACT is a national college admissions examination with subject areas in English, Math, Science, Reading, and sometimes writing.

test, the computer generates your score. So, the good news is that I knew right away what I'd scored. The bad news is that I knew right away that I'd scored poorly.

The score was actually barely above average, but in the world of pursuing a Ph.D. it was low. Too low, in my opinion - and I imagined in the opinion of the graduate school professors and committee - to be taken seriously. I'd scored so low that I was actually embarrassed to submit the scores to the graduate school. I had very confidently written them a letter letting them know that although I hadn't taken the test yet, I was confident that I would score highly. And I hadn't.

Still, I submitted the score to the school. I didn't email an excuse. I just emailed the score. I was hoping that the rest of my packet would make up for the epic fail of the GRE. Then I said a prayer to God reminding him about that whole "increase, overflow, and favor" thing - with favor being the operative word. After that, I sat back and waited.

Being in college full time, working on a senior honors thesis and also working full time made me quite busy. Before I knew it some time had passed and I hadn't heard anything back from the Ph.D. program. I assumed that I hadn't been invited for an interview just based on my GRE scores, and I couldn't say that I blamed them. That was a Friday.

That Monday, I decided I needed to know for sure so I called the department and spoke to the secretary. I told her that I had applied to the Ph.D. program and hadn't heard anything back. She informed me that they'd had 95 applicants and were only accepting 6, and not everyone would get a call back or an invitation to interview.

Inside I thought, 'Wow! I knew it! I knew I didn't make the cut!' Now, don't get me wrong, I was smart. I had always been smart. I was always at the top of my class, always on honor roll, and then later in college on president's lists and dean's lists every semester. But it was a Ph.D. program, for crying out loud. So simply being smart wouldn't be enough. I knew the best of the best would be applying, and I felt as if I'd ruined my chances with those GRE scores.

Still, the secretary took my name and said she'd check my status. Two minutes later she came back to the phone very excited. She proclaimed, "We have been emailing you for weeks! You were invited to the first round of interviews but you never responded to the email. The second and final round of interviews is next Monday. Can you make it?" I exclaimed, "Yes, I'll be there!" Then I apologized for not checking my email. She scheduled me for the following week's final interviews, and then we got off the phone.

Sure enough, when we got off the phone I ran over to my computer and there were three emails inviting me to interview for possible admittance into the program. And I had missed them all! The interview I missed would have been the previous Monday, and the next interview was the upcoming Monday. I excitedly called my mom who took off from work so she could make the drive with me to the school for the interview.

I thanked God for another chance at this thing, realizing that they could have just written me off after missing my email. I thanked Him for the opportunity to interview. The secretary had told me that they'd only invited 15 people to interview out of the 95 that applied. From the 15 interviewees I knew they would only pick 6. The pressure was on!

If you think the devil does not exist then you are wrong. He does not go down without a fight, and he pops up right as God is preparing to move you into your destiny. The devil might pop up with a phone call from an ex just as you and your spouse are having a hard time with things, or he might use someone close to you to invite the temptation into your life. He might try to interfere with you getting to church on a day there is a "word" earmarked for you and your deliverance.

The devil might mess with the hearts and minds of your children, irritate you on your job, or on your way home so that you invite animosity and irritation into your home and onto your family, thus ruining the flavor of your home, and keeping you from peace. For me he uses my lack of patience.

On the way to the University to interview for admittance into the Ph.D. program, I got in the wrong lane. My mom suggested we just get off at the next exit and turn around. I didn't want to waste the time so I tried to cut across the median, and wouldn't you know it?, I got stuck in the mud! We had to sit there for over an hour waiting for a tow truck to tow us out of the mud, and because it was after hours the "tow" - which took all of 8 minutes - cost $123.00!

I was beyond infuriated and irritated, and suggested we turn back. I was so annoyed that I didn't want to even go to the interview! My mom coaxed me into moving forward and not letting the devil get to me, and we proceeded. To this day, eight years later, I grimace when I think of that day, and that $123.00 bill!

We got there, behind schedule of course. We checked into our hotel (the interview was the next day, for the whole day). I showered and was out the door to a social the previous year's Ph.D. students were having. I arrived late but it went well.

The next day was "D" day, and as I walked to the campus I felt so good. This felt right. The campus was beautiful and picturesque and I knew that's where I wanted to be. I knew that's where I would be.

During the interviews, which were an hour long with each of the professors – one interview per person per professor - I was not nervous. Despite being thrown some tough scenarios and situations, as well as thought-provoking questions, I did great.

I did so well, in fact, that when all of us interviewees gathered back in the rooms together between the interview sessions, and many of the interviewees began talking about what they'd said wrong, or how they'd messed up, I didn't comment. Because I hadn't felt like I'd said "the wrong thing" or been stumped by a question.

When a fellow interviewee turned to me specifically and asked "How'd you do?" I said, "I did great! I know I'm in." I wasn't bragging, far from it. I just knew that I would be accepted. Up until that point, I had never felt more certain of anything in my life.

During those many breaks in which we interviewees gathered, sought refreshments and updates on how our fellow interviewees were faring, we learned a lot about each other. The person who had turned to me and asked me how I'd done had already earned two Master's degrees. Another person had a perfect score on the GRE and had conducted international research. As a matter of fact, he had just flown in from another country to interview for this program!

Still, others had much more experience than I had, or more degrees, and surely most if not all of them had higher GRE scores. Yet I remained unfazed. I knew this program was mine. I had a peace about the whole situation, (in hindsight I realize it was God's grace) and I just knew I was in.

That is, until the drive home. The devil reared his ugly head again and caused doubt to enter my mind. I wondered if I'd done as well as I'd thought. I remembered that guy with the perfect GRE scores, and then I remembered my lackluster score. I remembered the lady who'd already earned two Master's degrees, and I had none. I was still months away from even earning my Bachelor's degree.

I thought about better ways I could have said some things. I thought about some things I maybe shouldn't have said. For example, should I have so boldly professed my faith? Maybe that turned some people off. The social from the night before with the students who were already in the program revealed that at least one of the professors was an atheist. I didn't know which one. What if I offended whoever that was? Should I have done some things differently?

I realized that there wasn't much I would have changed. And thanks to my mom, I realized the futility of worrying about something I couldn't control (which is something I struggle with to this day, I am a worrywart), so I reluctantly decided that what was done was done (mom's words) and that there wasn't anything more I could do. I decided that God would have to take it from there.

The next day, a Tuesday, I jumped on the computer to work on my senior honors thesis. I had been working several hours when the phone rang. It was noon. I answered the phone and it was a professor from the Ph.D. department of the school where I had just interviewed. Specifically, it was the professor who had similar research interests as mine[18]. She was calling me to let me know that I was the first student they were calling to let know that they'd been accepted into the Ph.D. program! I had been accepted!

Out of 95 applicants, and 15 interviewees, I would be one of the six that got into this program! And to top it all off, I was the first one they'd called to give the news to!

I screamed! I mean, I let it rip right into the phone (with the professor still on the line). Then I dropped the phone, still screaming, and ran down the stairs, still screaming!

It took me a minute to realize three things. First, I was home alone, so there was no one to share the

[18] And I later found out the professor with similar research interests as mine was the atheist. Doesn't God have a great sense of humor?

news with. Second, that I would need to call my family so I could share the news with them. Then, third, that I was already on the phone, so I couldn't place a call. And that's when it hit me! I was already on the phone! The professor was still on the phone! I had dropped the phone (with her still on it) and had run downstairs, forgetting that she was still on the line!

Just to be clear, first I had assaulted her ears with a blood-curdling scream, then I had dropped the phone with her still on it and ran downstairs!

As soon as I realized my blunder, I ran back up the stairs and was relieved to find her calling my name and laughing on the other end. I apologized profusely for the scream and for dropping the phone. She accepted my apology. Laughed some more. Congratulated me some more. And with shaky hands I dialed my parents and family to tell them the good news!

Despite my subpar GRE scores, despite the fact that I probably wasn't the most qualified, or the smartest student, or even that I'd missed the email alerting me to my invitation to interview, or that I'd missed the first round of interviews, or that I almost missed the application deadline in the first place, God allowed everything to come together in my favor and I was accepted into that Ph.D. program. That is what Favor looks like!

But God wasn't done with me yet.

In addition to getting accepted into the program, He allowed for my full tuition to be paid and for me to be paid a salary over and above what I had been making as a hotel front desk clerk, and for even fewer hours worked. It's called a fellowship, and is awarded by a university or by departments within a university.

A fellowship allows doctoral students to work just a few hours per week either as a Graduate Research Assistant (which I was) or a Graduate Teaching Assistant, but to be paid a small salary in addition to having their full tuition paid. For example, whereas I used to work 40 or more hours for a couple hundred dollars per week as a front desk hotel clerk, I was now making a few hundred dollars per week for 10-15 hours of work. The University and/or their departments had GRAs and GTAs work so few hours because it was understood that a student's studies would be challenging and were the priority.

The way that I got my fellowship was yet another blessing from God. As you know, I barely made the application deadline, which didn't give me a lot of time to seek out possible fellowships or assistantships. The program director called me at 11 p.m. one night at my home to tell me of a fellowship for which I was qualified. He told me the deadline expired the next day and had me send over all the materials he requested.

I emailed the information, and the information I couldn't email I faxed. And sure enough, I was awarded the fellowship. To reiterate, I would now be making double the money for working less than half of the hours, and that didn't even include the fact that I was also having my full tuition paid. That's what I call Increase!

But God was STILL not done with me.

And if you think the initial circumstance in which God demonstrated Favor, or the subsequent circumstance in which God demonstrated Increase was something, prepare to be blown away. This one takes the cake.

In my last semester of college, after I'd been accepted into the Ph.D. program, and after I'd been awarded the highly coveted four-year fellowship, with only a month or two left before I graduated college, I received a check in the mail. The check was for over $4,000 made payable to me from a source I didn't recognize. It had the name of the University I was attending and due to graduate from in the next couple months in the top, left-hand corner, so I called my University to see what that money was about and where it came from.

I have to be honest and admit that somewhere inside I thought about not making that call. I did not want someone somewhere to realize the error and take back that check. I figured the check was a mistake. And if I wanted to keep that mistake to myself, I figured I'd better just cash it and not draw any attention to it.

But I didn't do that. I decided to call and inquire about the check for two reasons. One, I knew better. I did not want to lose any blessings doing the wrong thing, just to keep a few extra dollars. Even though they were A LOT of extra dollars!

Second, I didn't want the school to come looking for me once they discovered they'd accidentally paid me four grand. Four thousand dollars is a lot of money to get, but it's also a lot of money to have to pay back. I didn't want to acquire that money fraudulently and lose blessings, and I didn't want to have to pay it back if it was an error.

So, I called my school's financial aid department and explained that I had received a check for over $4,000 and I wasn't sure why. They looked into it, and reported back to me that it was not an error. The financial aid manager got on the phone and told me that the over $4,000 check was indeed mine, and that it was sent to me because I had received a grant that had not been paid out.

FYI: I had never applied for any grant! Never! Not once during my whole four years of college had I applied for a grant, yet here was a "grant" that I had received, payable in full to me.

When I told the financial aid manager that I hadn't applied for a grant she told me, "Well, it seems as though you've received one. Congratulations!" I was shocked. I asked her at least three or four times if I would have to pay it back, in any way, at any time. She assured me each and every one of those times that I would not. That grants were not loans and did not have to be paid back.

That is when my shock turned into awe. I was awed by the power of God. I was in awe of the way He blessed. I was in awe that His idea of Overflow for a 22 year-old young woman was a random, unexpected check for $4,000 (when I would have been more than satisfied with $400, maybe even $40).

I was awed by the reach of His Favor. I was awed that His Favor could reach professors and program directors, atheists, even check-writers.

I was awed by the depths of his Increase. From January to May I had experienced "Increase, Overflow, and Favor" which were exactly what I'd prayed for, but so much more than I could have expected.

And here's some surprising news. I am not special. God did not do this for me because I am so wonderful. Nor did He do it because I deserved those things. As I've said before I have a temper that I have to constantly pray about. And I have sinned and fallen short of His glory on far too many occasions to count. God did this for me because that's what He does - when you obey Him. When you submit to His will, when you live for Him, He shows out and shows off in your life and blesses beyond your wildest imagination.

That's just the kind of God He is. That's just the kind of God we serve. He is still very much in the blessing business. Try Him.

Testimony 7: God Uses Whomever He Needs to Bless Whomever He Wants

My maternal grandmother tells a story of something she experienced as a young woman. Although as a child I found the story eerie, I have come to see its value and understand its significance.

My maternal grandparents had 11 children. My grandfather was a longshoreman, and my grandmother was a nurse's aide (currently called a nurse's assistant). With that many mouths to feed, money and resources were sometimes scarce, but my grandmother never feared or worried. She always looked to God "from whence cometh her help" (Psalm 121:1). My grandmother is 86 and that is still one of her favorite scriptures.

After my grandfather fought in World War II he wasn't quite the same. He became an alcoholic, and much of the responsibility for providing for their children (and for him) fell on my grandmother's shoulders.

On a Friday in August, when my grandmother was in her early 30's, she went to the mailbox and found an eviction letter. She and my grandfather were buying their home, but had been 3 months late with their $65 house note. My grandmother recalled how she'd only had enough money to feed her children just a little bit, and not much more.

The letter in the mailbox was to let her know that she and her family would be evicted that Monday at 12 p.m. if the late house payments were not made. She was also warned that the bank was going to put all of her family's belongings out of the house and onto the street.

My grandmother retrieved the letter, read it, folded it and put it away so she could proceed with her daily routine. Because it was summertime and very hot (August), my grandmother's children were out of school, and she would always call them in at noon from playing in the yard, give them baths to cool them off, and then have them take their afternoon nap lying on top of a thin blanket on the living room floor.

She had them lay together on the living room floor so they could all share the one fan in the house, an old oscillating fan, their only reprieve from those southern summers.

After the kids had fallen asleep, my grandmother went into her bedroom and closed the door. The window was open. She kneeled down in her bedroom, took out the eviction letter, and said her prayers.

She held the eviction letter in her hands and poured her heart out to God. She first thanked Him for all of His blessings, and then she asked for some help. She told God that she had received an eviction notice and was in fear of losing her home and not having a place for her children to go. She said, "Lord, you see this letter. I have nowhere to bring my children, and my husband won't help. Lord, I don't want my children to be put out on the street." She said a few more things in her prayer to God, all while holding that eviction notice.

No sooner had she finished her prayer that there was a knock on the door. She went to the door and saw a lady standing there at the bottom of her stairs in a white uniform with buttons up the front of her dress. The lady said, "Hello. I'm mama Quill." My grandmother said, "Hello." The strange lady then proceeded to walk up the front stairs, past my grandmother and right into her house.

My grandmother remembers being taken aback by the lady, and the fact that she had walked right into her home. The children were all asleep on the floor, and the lady, "Ms. Quill" commented, "What beautiful children you have here." She then went around the room laying hands on each of their foreheads.

Ms. Quill then stood up abruptly, and said, "Now what's wrong? What happened?" My grandmother, not wanting to tell a perfect stranger her business, said, "Nothing." Ms. Quill said, "Tell me what happened. God don't send Ms. Quill nowhere for nothing. God told me to come to this house."

With embarrassment my grandmother finally told the stranger, Ms. Quill, that she was late on house payments and was going to be evicted on Monday. Ms. Quill sat down, took out a pen and her checkbook and began writing a check. Seconds later she stopped writing, inhaled sharply, and said, "Ohhh", as if she was responding to something someone said. She then tore up the check she had been writing and rewrote a new check.

When she was finished writing the check she turned to my grandmother and said, "Now mama Quill paid your three months behind and one month ahead for you. When you get the money, you pay mama Quill back." Ms. Quill then walked right out the door. My grandmother had never seen that lady before that day!

About a week or two later, school started for the children, and my grandmother would walk them to school every day. On one of their walks to school, sitting there on the side of the street in a candy truck was Ms. Quill. My grandmother would later learn that Ms. Quill was the "candy store lady" that used to sell candy and sweets out of her truck.

When my grandmother saw Ms. Quill she thought, *Wow, that's the lady that helped me that day.* She then walked up to her and said "Hello." Ms. Quill said, "What you got for Ms. Quill?" My grandmother had $2.00 on her, which she gave to Ms. Quill. Everyday my grandmother would pass Ms. Quill and whether or not she had any money she would say "Hello." Ms. Quill would ask, "What you got for me?", and my grandmother would give what she could.

I cannot help but wonder how many of us would have "ducked" Ms. Quill, especially if we didn't have the money to pay her back. And some of us probably would have "ducked" her even if we did have the money.

For her part, Ms. Quill never gave my grandmother a hard time when she could only pay back a few dollars, nor when she had no money at all to give. Still, little by little my grandmother paid Ms. Quill until she had paid her back all the money. She says she knows God sent that lady to her door!

Because of my grandmother's prayers, God had sent Ms. Quill to her door with a blessing. And because Ms. Quill was obedient to God, she allowed herself to be used to bless a family in need and keep them off the streets.

God still hears AND ANSWERS prayers! By any means necessary He will use whomever and whatever He has to bless you! He is still a God of unconventional miracles.

Testimony 8: God Protects Us, Even From Ourselves

I had just purchased a pre-owned (used), cherry-red BMW 328ic. The convertible sports car was a gift I'd bought for myself to celebrate my accomplishments, which included graduating from college with honors, and then being accepted into a competitive graduate school doctoral program with a fellowship that paid all of my tuition as well as a stipend (a small salary).

When school started, I jumped in, hitting the books as hard as I'd done in college, not really stopping to "smell the coffee" (I prefer to smell coffee over roses). So a couple years after being in the Ph.D. program, after a particularly grueling semester was successfully completed, I'd figured now was as good a time as ever, and I decided to buy myself a convertible.

I wanted a convertible because I wanted to put my top down and cruise along with my music on the long drives home to visit my family during school breaks.

I researched various convertibles, and settled on a Chevy Camaro. It had low miles, its VIN[19] number checked out, and it was super affordable, having been priced well below the Kelley Blue Book (KBB) value.

When I arrived at the dealership, sure enough, there sat the convertible Camaro I had researched and decided upon. However, next to it sat a car that caught my eye, and my heart. It was the used BMW that I mentioned, and although it was a bit more expensive than the Camaro, I was instantly in love, and decided I wanted it. I talked to the salesman, test drove the car, got the information on it, including its price, and then I left.

When I got home I researched the vehicle and found that it was highly-rated, considered safe, and its VIN number also checked out. What didn't check out, however, was the price. The salesman had the car priced much higher than what it was worth, by KBB standards, so with the KBB printout in-hand, I went back out there seeking to negotiate.

Negotiations went well. The salesman honored the price I requested and I bought the car. This was my newest used car ever! And I was so excited to show

[19] Vehicle Identification Number.

my family, as I had not told them I'd bought a new(er) car.

The following weekend, I loaded up my new car with my luggage, some new CDs, and sunglasses, and set out on the drive to see my family. En route there was no traffic, and even though I know that I'm not supposed to speed, I was curious to see what my new car could do.

Let me tell you, it could get up and go! I accelerated and was amazed at its speed, and impressed with its smooth handling. Having gotten my need for speed out of the way, I settled back into the speed limit.

About two hours later I ran into a bit of traffic, and it slowed me down considerably. It also delayed my scheduled arrival time and made me feel as if I needed to make up the time I'd lost.

Up ahead was a bridge, so I decided to "gun it" over the bridge and make up some lost time that way. About a quarter of the way up the bridge there was a car in front of me which forced me to slow down, so I attempted to get over into the next lane so that I could resume my speed.

I got over, but before I could accelerate again, a car from the left lane jumped in front of me, and rather annoyingly drove side-by-side with the car that had previously been in front of me. Both of these cars, riding side-by-side, and thus taking up both lanes on the bridge, kept me from going around and thus speeding up.

I slowly rode behind them, fuming all the way. When I got to the other side of the bridge, still with those same two cars in front of me, I was surprised to find a police car, hiding behind a sign, waiting for a speeding driver.

If not for the "slow drivers" ahead of me, forcing me to slow down, I would have surely been that speeding driver the police officer was waiting for and would have likely had my car impounded (considering the speed I was going). At a minimum I would have been ticketed a large sum of money, as well as additional charges for reckless driving.

More importantly, by making me slow down, that could have possibly saved my life or someone else's. I could have lost control of my car and hit or killed someone, or my car could've flipped and killed me.

I believe that God allowed those drivers to block my way, forcing me to slow down. That whole ordeal scared me so much that I have never sped again. I have been driving for 15 years, and I have never received a speeding ticket. Ever. As a matter of fact, I am now one of those people who will hunk at others who speed!

In addition to bestowing His grace and favor on me that day, God taught me a valuable lesson. I learned that when we ask Him to lead and guide us, He will.

Testimony 9: God Blesses in Unexpected Ways

When my grandmother died, suddenly, the whole family was devastated, and I was no exception. I had spent my childhood summers at my grandmother's house[20], and I brokenheartedly thought back to those days spent on her front stoop eating watermelon, or in her kitchen watching the "stories[21]".

She had given me my first taste of coffee, and we would sit back and watch her morning stories, each with our own cup of "coffee". Even though my cup of coffee consisted mostly of milk and about a teaspoon of her coffee poured in, I still felt so important, so grown-up, and so incredibly special. My grandmother had a way of making those around her feel that way.

My grandmother lived very far away, over 1,200 miles from where I lived, and I have always been afraid of heights, so my husband and I knew we were not going to fly. Our options were to drive or take the train, but either way we both knew that

---

[20] See Testimony #10.

[21] The Young and the Restless, mainly.

the trip to attend my grandmother's funeral would take at least two days each way and would be expensive.

It is common knowledge that when you make arrangements for a trip early, you get certain discounts. But with an unexpected death, we did not have that luxury. So we settled for what we could get.

We initially tried to reserve train tickets (which would save us from having to make that long drive with our young children), but the train was booked. So we prepared ourselves for the two-day drive.

The night before we were supposed to leave, my husband and I did not get nearly as much done as we'd thought we would. It dawned on us that we would still be preparing for our trip even on the day we were due to leave, which would make us fall behind schedule even more than we already knew we would (traveling with young children causes one to automatically expect delays).

So, on a whim, the night before we were due to leave town, I called the train station to see if any seats had opened up, and they were still all booked. Exhausted, we went to bed and set our alarm clock to wake up early so we could get some more packing done, run some last-minute errands, and hopefully hit the road only a few hours past our schedule.

Not surprisingly, we woke up as exhausted as we'd gone to bed, and the thought of driving seemed like torture. Again, on a whim, and after a quick prayer, I called the train station, and was excited (and thankful) to find that the necessary seats had opened up. My family and I had been saved from making that dreaded two-day drive and would be able to take the train all the way to our destination and back (blessing #1).

We were quoted a price, a bereavement fare, and we booked it and with relief prepared for the train ride. We were even a bit happy because we knew our four year-old would really love riding the train. He always does.

About 30 minutes after we booked the train, I called the train station with a question. After the attendant put in my reservation number as a reference to answer my question, it was soon discovered that there had been a glitch in the system that had caused our fare to be hundreds of dollars less than what it should've been (blessing #2). Because we had already booked the train, the fare was honored. We were saved hundreds of dollars!

Although we were running late (as we tend to do with little ones) we were able to make the train with seconds to spare (blessing #3) and we boarded the train without incident. We settled in and, as we expected, our oldest son was blissfully happy to be on the train, and we were too, because we had been able to avoid that drive.

A couple hours into our ride we were notified that our infant would not actually be able to ride free as we'd been told. He would have to ride on our laps all the way there. We wondered how he'd sleep comfortably. Surely we weren't expected to let him sleep in our arms? What if he rolled out of our arms as we slept? What if the train had an accident?

As a mom, I was instantly worried, but there was nothing we could do. We couldn't even buy an extra seat because the train was full.

To make matters worse, a group of young men and a young woman got on the train, and they were cursin'[22] up a storm (like my grandmother would say). In our home we do not use profanity. And we

[22] Using profanity.

do not want our son exposed to such language. But this was a public space, so we were limited in controlling the environment.

It is unfortunate that in this day and age, we cannot expect adults to be mindful of children being around, and to govern themselves accordingly. Nowadays respect is just too much to ask.

Thankfully, during the group's "colorful" conversation, my son was watching a movie on his portable DVD player, but we knew that would not be the case during the entire train ride (and they were going as far as we were on the train). So we decided to ask about getting private sleeping quarters on the train.

Private sleeping quarters on the train, also called a bedroom or a sleeper, is a wonderful thing. Depending on the size of the room you buy, you get a full bathroom with shower, or at least a private toilet, as well as a fold down bed, adjustable room thermostat, and all meals included.

Because there were four of us, we would need the full bedroom (we weren't allowed to get anything smaller). We knew it would be a wonderful thing to get a bedroom, but we also knew it was out of our price range. We had already inquired about the cost, and because there were no bereavement fares that included a bedroom, we would lose the bereavement discount, and an additional $1,000 would be added to the price of our tickets.

Still, the fact that it was out of our price range didn't even matter, because the sleepers had been sold out when we asked about them while we were making our original reservation.

But we decided to try again. We asked the train's car attendant if a bedroom was available and she said "No, maybe later." We waited an hour then asked a second person, and they also said that no bedroom was available. We waited again, and asked again, and this time we were told "I don't know if a bedroom is available." We were told to try back in 30 minutes.

Meanwhile we went to dinner (you pay out of pocket when you don't have a room). Thirty minutes later, as expected, we went to see the train conductor and were told that there was a bedroom available (blessing #4). I was ecstatic! My children would be able to rest comfortably, and away from our boisterous and disrespectful seatmates.

My husband, although also happy, was a bit skeptical. He reserved his celebration until we found out what the bedroom would cost. Having already been quoted a $1600 price tag, $800 alone for the bedroom, he was understandably leery. My husband asked, "How much is the bedroom?" The conductor looked at his sheet and said "$241" The price for the bedroom was now over one-third less than it had originally been quoted (blessing #5).

This made my husband excited, and when we got to the bedroom my son said "Wow!" His "wow" definitely summed up the experience. Not only had we been given the bedroom, we had been given the deluxe bedroom, which included separate bathroom with shower, as well as extra leg room and space (blessing #6). We had the kind of extra space that was perfect for a four year-old, not to mention his parents!

Yet the blessings didn't stop there. When we got to town, we were surprised with a rental car (blessing #7), without having to pay for it. On the way into town, as well as from the time we had learned about my grandmother's death, we had been in prayer. We prayed for traveling grace and mercy, and most importantly we prayed for God's grace on my family.

We knew that a lot of people would take my grandmother's untimely departure really hard, so we prayed that they would be comforted.

The day before the funeral we were able to connect with some family members we had not seen in a long time, as well as a few new family members. My sons got to meet some new cousins and there was joy, as we all reconnected.

During the funeral, as could be expected, it was tough. My family was understandably grief-stricken, and the tears flowed freely. But after the funeral, as we all gathered to share a meal and memories of my grandmother, I was able to look around and see so much love within the family and even among the friends and associates that had gathered to pay their condolences and show their support.

Even after the repass[23], we all gathered at my grandmother's house and the energy was electric. There were family members on the porch laughing, like old times; children were in the yard running

---

[23] A repass refers to the gathering of a deceased person's family and friends following their funeral, where the family and friends come together to share a meal and memories of their time with their deceased loved one. It is also a time to "catch up" with family members you may not have seen in a while.

around and playing ball, like old times; family members were gathered around the dining room table, in the living room, in the kitchen, and in the backyard, all laughing, reminiscing, and enjoying each other, like old times.

At one point, I remember looking up towards heaven and thinking to myself that my grandmother was probably enjoying herself most of all. I knew that she was looking down on us, proud that we were her family, and that we were there enjoying each other in her honor.

On that day, even in the midst of loss, God got the glory. Even though we didn't know why God had chosen to take my grandmother, we knew that He used everything for His glory. My grandmother's passing brought glory to God because so many of us were able to come together and fellowship and witness to one another about God's goodness. Even in the midst of our sadness.

At my grandmother's funeral, people who had not even personally met her were moved to stand and speak about the powerful presence of God, or the love they felt that day in the church.

There was laughter and joy, even in the midst of the sadness, and I was reminded of the scripture that says, "I will give you peace that surpasses all understanding" (Philippians 4:7). I had witnessed love, joy, and peace, at a funeral no less, and I knew it could only be God.

And wouldn't you know it? We were also blessed to get another sleeper for the return trip (and again for less than we should've had to pay!)

Most importantly, God is getting the glory from this whole situation, many times over, because I am able to share His goodness with you!

Testimony 10: God Heals Broken Hearts

Less than a handful of people know this story.

When I was 12 years old, my parents split up. My parents had been high school sweethearts, and I could still remember the loving note that my mom had left on the inside cover of my dad's yearbook when she was a sophomore and he was a senior in high school, about to graduate. It spoke of the love she had for him and the anticipation of them spending their lives together.

My brothers and I thought our parents would be together forever. Everyone did. Our house had been the place where all our friends and cousins hung out. Whether having water balloon fights, playing videogames, playing basketball in the backyard, or laughing on the seesaw my dad had built, we were always together having fun, laughing, playing.

No one saw their split coming. At least not my brothers and I. One day we were a family, and the next day (or so it seems) they were sitting us down and telling us that they were no longer going to be married and asking us who, between the two of them, we wanted to live with.

I was devastated, as were my brothers. My parents, together, were all we'd ever known. And I wanted it to stay that way.

Only twelve at that time, I got the brilliant idea that if I just killed myself, and left a note for my parents telling them that my death wish was for them to get back together, that they would have to honor it. And my brothers, at least, would get to have my parents back together.

So, I made a plan. I decided that I would swallow a ton of pills and do it that way. I just needed the perfect opportunity to do it, so I sat back and waited for one[24].

---

[24] Suicide (killing yourself) is NOT the answer! Killing yourself is NEVER the answer to any problem. EVER. I know now, and found out very soon after initially feeling as hopeless as I did when my parents split up, that killing myself would not have solved my problem nor gotten my parents back together. As a matter of fact, it likely would have made their relationship worse, as well as destroyed the lives of my siblings (who I thought I was trying to help in the first place). Also, it would have permanently taken me away, so that I wouldn't have had a chance to see things get better. Problems and hopeless situations ALWAYS get better. Sometimes, they even get better than they originally were. Those hopeless situations and problems can actually turn out to be blessings in disguise. As for me, my parents splitting up was a definite blessing in disguise because my dad is ultra-protective (read: a little crazy) as it concerns dating. Although my daddy is the sweetest man in the world, a big ole' teddy bear, being that I was the only girl in a home with all brothers, he was very strict about dating. (He once told me that I could date when I was married,

Testimony

We used to spend our summer days at my paternal grandmother's house, while my parents worked. We'd be outside eating watermelon trying to cool off during those humid summer days, or racing each other around the block to see who was the fastest, or inside having dancing competitions and playing bingo, or the card game UNO.

One day my grandmother and I were sitting in the kitchen and she was cooking. Without meaning to, I started to cry. I had been trying to conceal the pain I was feeling from my parents' separation, and on that day in the kitchen with my grandmother, by the grace of God, it all came spilling out.

I confided in my grandmother that I had planned to kill myself so that my parents would have to get back together. My grandmother turned her pot of food off, sat me down next to her and immediately started talking to me about God.

---

and he didn't crack a smile). Having my dad out of the home at least allowed me to date before I turned 30 ☺. It was bad enough that I had to "sneak" to the movies with a boy even after mom gave permission. Can you imagine how much worse it would have been with my dad down the hallway?! See, God really does work everything out for the good of those who love Him ☺. But, all jokes aside, there are others way to get your parents' attention. Start by talking to them and telling them how you feel. If that doesn't work, talk to God. But no matter what, DO NOT make a permanent decision about a temporary situation. Live to see it change.

My grandmother told me that God had plans for my life, and that He wanted me here. She told me that although she knew it was hard for me, that God would handle it. She said He'd fight this battle for me and would get me through. She then played Yolanda Adams' song "The battle is not yours, it's the Lord's", and we had us a good ole' bible study right there in the kitchen.

After that day, we would sit for hours talking about God, with "The Battle is not yours" playing in the background, on repeat, as I listened and cried. My grandmother, Florence, would let me cry on her shoulder, and she would sit and talk to me for hours about God "being able to get me through anything" or "fighting my battles for me."

Since I didn't know how to fight having my world turned upside down by divorce, I decided I would try God out for myself. I would ask Him to "fight" this battle for me.

I prayed, tentatively at first, then with more conviction. I prayed that my parents would get back together, that something would happen to me, thus prompting them to get back together. I prayed that my heart would heal. I prayed that the anger would go away (around that time I started to get into a lot of fights) and despite being the

Valedictorian of my 8th grade class, I was warned that if I got into one more fight I would be expelled. But still I continued to try this prayer thing.

I prayed, cried, and prayed some more.

My grandmother continued to counsel me over the next several weeks. Every day she would talk to me about God's grace, about His goodness and how He could and would see me through this difficult time. Over time the desire to kill myself went away as I truly started to believe that God would fight this "battle" for me.

In the years since, I've come to understand that God was already fighting that battle for me through my grandmother. Little did I know, that time she spent with me eighteen years ago, talking to me about God's goodness, His grace and mercy, not only saved my life, but it set the foundation for my faith; a faith that continues -strong and bold, though not without trials – to this day.

My grandmother saved my life in that kitchen, but she also introduced me, for the first time, to God's goodness.

My grandmother Florence passed away this year, after church, on a Sunday in July, and I know that she is with God right now and He is telling her "Job well done."

Postface

How to access God

Well, you've read the *Testimony* book and, I pray, are moved to want to seek a relationship with God.

It could be that you already had a relationship with God and want to renew it. It could be because you want to experience some of the blessings and miracles discussed in this book. Or, it could be because you're just curious about how this whole "God" thing works. Or it could be none of the above.

Whatever the reason, we have come to perhaps the most interesting part of this book, the place where we ask "How do we access God and unleash His blessings and miracles in our lives?"

Well, the answer is quite easy. We access God through prayer. When we pray to Him we talk to Him. Prayer is not a complicated thing. And it doesn't have to be as theatrical as what you may have seen in church or on TV. Prayer is simply going before God with a humble and open heart.

A good guideline for prayer can be found in Matthew 6:9-13. Actually, all of Matthew 6 is a great resource for how to pray, and includes helpful information such as why you should not say the same things over and over during prayer, and the importance of forgiving others, so you should certainly check it out.

But Matthew 6:9-13 is a complete one-stop-shop prayer, and includes acknowledgement of God, praise of Him, asking Him to lead and guide us, asking for what we need to survive, as well as a plea for forgiveness and a request for protection. It ends with another acknowledgement of Him. It has all the ingredients and is stated as follows:

> "After this manner therefore pray ye:
> 'Our Father which art in heaven, Hallowed be they name.
> Thy kingdom come. Thy will be done in earth, as it is in heaven.
> Give us this day our daily bread.
> And forgive us our debts, as we forgive our debtors.
> And lead us not into temptation, but deliver us from evil: For thine is the kingdom, and the power, and the glory, forever. Amen.'" (KJV)

That was the King James Version. I like this version because it allows me to read the words as close to their true form as possible. I also like to read more modern versions so that I can "see" what the words mean with present-day wording. The New International Version is stated as follows:

"This, then, is how you should pray:
'Our Father in heaven,
Hallowed be your name,
Your kingdom come
Your will be done,
On earth as it is in heaven
Give us today our daily bread.
And forgive us our debts,
As we also have forgiven our debtors.
And lead us not into temptation,
But deliver us from the evil one'" (NIV)

Simplified further, the Our Father Prayer says:

God, you are our Father, and you are in Heaven,
Your name is Holy,
The end of the world will one day come,
So have your way with me
Here on earth as well as in heaven
Feed and provide for me today
Forgive all the money I owe to others
And I will forgive those who owe me
Lead me away from bad things
Keep me safe from the devil
For heaven and the world are yours
You have all the power and you get all the glory forever
Amen

The Our Father prayer is a good place to start, if you need someplace to start. However, your prayer doesn't have to be anything formal or memorized. It is an honest talk to, and with, God. It bares your soul.

We can lie to a lot of people but we cannot lie to Him. It is a good idea to ask for forgiveness for our sins, so that we can come before Him fresh. Think about asking for forgiveness kind of like cleaning the lenses of God's glasses, so He can see you better, clearer, without the obstruction of our sins blinding Him from seeing our hearts.

Or think of it like washing your hands before you eat your meal. Washing your hands (asking for forgiveness) allows you to enjoy your meal (talk to God/ receive blessings) without having your dirt (sins) taint your meal (blessings/prayer life).

It is a good idea to ask for forgiveness even for sins you are unaware of, or didn't express outwardly. For example, ask for forgiveness even if you've only had sinful thoughts, or were unaware that you had lied about something. It just gives us a clean, fresh slate on which to begin our prayer. Forgiveness is like a clean, fresh, sheet of paper (before you begin writing).

It is also a good idea to acknowledge and praise Him in your prayer. God is like a parent. He wants so much for us, literally "every good thing", but He expects certain things from us too.

Are you a parent, or an aunt, or uncle? Are you a grandparent, a friend, a human being? Have you ever given something to someone and regretted it because they were ungrateful? Thankfully God is so much better than us, and is not petty or governed by feelings, but I imagine He would still appreciate our acknowledgment of the things He does for us.

"Thank you" is a great way to acknowledge Him and it also serves as a great reminder of how good He has already been. Even if you feel that he has not done much for you, the fact that you are breathing, living, even reading this book or having it read to you signifies that you have been blessed. You have been given the gift of life. A gift that for far too many people has expired and often sooner than what they might have hoped.

Use your gift wisely, use your life wisely, and make the most of it. Pray and talk to God, follow His commandments (attached as an endnote[i] at the end of this book on the very last page), and try to live a good life. Be truthful, loving, kind to others, help those in need, forgive others even as you ask for forgiveness for yourself, and pray.

It's as simple as that. It's not easy, but it is simple. Your prayer doesn't have to be an hour or even 5 minutes. It doesn't have to be on your knees, or in the back of a church.

Your prayer can be a few seconds in your car on your way to work, or school, or it can occur as you open your eyes in the morning or as you close them at night.

Encourage prayer among your family, friends, even strangers if you feel moved to. Just like we would want to share good news and great things with the people we love, why not share the best thing – the power of prayer?

Prayer can give and get the people we love so much more than we can, so why not share this incredibly great thing with them? Prayer for our loved ones – our mothers, fathers, sons, daughters, grandparents, aunts, uncles, cousins, friends, colleagues - and encouraging them to pray for themselves is the best gift we can give them. And it's the best gift we can get from them. Plus, it's free! So, try it today. It is guaranteed to work.

How to hear from God

Praying to God is our way of talking to Him. Prayer allows us to talk to Him about how we feel, what we need, our concerns, fears, whatever is going on in our lives. But reading our bible allows us to hear from Him.

When we read His word, we hear from Him about His needs, what He wants for our lives, and how He wants us to live. The bible gives us answers to our questions, it alleviates fears we hold in our hearts, as well as anger, and other things we struggle to overcome. It can even guide us through life's issues, big and small.

I have sought God on questions of who to date, if and when to get married, what school to attend, which house to buy (as well as help to be able to buy one in the first place).

I have sought Him in His word about His promises to lead, guide, and protect my family and me. I have sought Him and called Him on His promises to heal when my mom was diagnosed with Breast Cancer and when my son was born 3 months early.

I have sought His counsel on why I was robbed at gunpoint and why my parents divorced. I have sought Him in my quest to escape hurt, harm, danger, and even traffic!

Reading the bible and learning His word allows us to call Him on what He may have said in His word (the bible). Like a child would say to a parent, we can say to God, "Remember when you promised this...?", and, "You said if I do this you would do that", and He honors those things He said He would do. He doesn't always honor what we tell Him to do, or what we want Him to do. Without fail, however, He absolutely, positively, always honors what He says.

But first you have to learn what He says. And to do that you have to read your bible.

Praying and reading the bible doesn't keep all of our problems away (obviously, or else I wouldn't have had a preemie son or a mom with Breast Cancer, or a dad with a heart attack, or been robbed at gunpoint). What prayer and reading the bible does is bless us with God's grace and mercy and favor, so that when we come up against life's issues, we have help dealing with them.

When we lose someone we have comfort. When we are involved in a traumatic situation we have God's grace to get us through it. When we come up against those unimaginable things we have assurance that God loves us and will not give us more than we can handle, and that through it all He will love, care, and comfort us. And He will pay us back for our obedience to Him, and for our commitment to living a life that will make Him proud.

If you want answers, guidance, or even just the peace that comes along with a relationship with God, then try reading your bible. It works, and it too is guaranteed.

May God bless you and your family!

And from our family, "**Welcome to the wonderfully powerful world of prayer!**"

If you have a testimony and would like to share it with others, and maybe even have it included in forthcoming books, please read the disclaimer[25], and then email it to:

info@ttppublishing.com.

Please put the word "TESTIMONY" in the subject line.

---

[25] DISCLAIMER: By submitting your testimony to us, you give us full permission, with all rights and privileges included, to use your testimony in future books, in magazine articles or on our website. We will only display the information you provide in your story, and considering the large audience we have, we encourage you NOT to post personal information. If you want your first name included in the testimony, please let us know and we will accommodate your request. If you want to remain anonymous, please state that and we will accommodate that request as well. We do not offer compensation for testimonies because we want to make sure the stories submitted are real and true and are not submitted to gain financial compensation. Thank you for submitting your testimony. We pray that it blesses the lives of others and that you are blessed in return.

About TTP Publishing

"Providing short and sweet books you can enjoy, when you're ready to enjoy them, that WON'T take all day...

...BECAUSE YOU HAVE THINGS TO DO."

TTP Publishing is a book and media publishing company that specializes in publishing short books. It was founded by an avid reader who, after becoming a mom, doctor, bill-payer, and errand-runner, realized she had little to no time left in a day to sit back and enjoy a good book.

What's more, this busy mom was also impatient, meaning she not only wanted to sit back and enjoy a good book with her limited "me" time, but she also wanted to reach the conclusion of that book - without having to wait days or even weeks before she had more time to read again.

This busy mom had an "aha" moment as she thought of how awesome it would be if good books were shorter and lasted the length of say, a good movie, or dinner out.

That's when **TTP Publishing** - "TTP" stands for **to the point** - was founded.

TTP's books are sometimes funny, sometimes controversial, sometimes spicy, and sometimes tell-it-like-it-is, but they are almost always short and to the point...*because you have things to do.*

For information on submitting your book for publication, please visit us at www.ttppublishing.com, or send us an email to info@ttppublishing.com.

Happy Reading!!!

TTP Publishing Books

Act Like a CEO, Think Like a Millionaire: Why You Should Care LESS About What a Man or Woman Thinks About Love, Relationships, Intimacy and Commitment and MORE About GETTING WHAT YOU WANT OUT OF LIFE

What You WON'T Expect When You're Expecting Because This is The CRAP They Don't Tell You: ABC's of a Sucky Pregnancy

Confessions of a Surrogate for Celebrities

TESTIMONY: 10 Stories Detailing Supernatural Miracles, Blessings, and THE POWER OF PRAYER

Open Marriage: An Erotic Trilogy (Book 1)

Open Marriage: A.S.E. Sports Agency (Book 2)

Open Marriage: Behind the Scenes (Book 3)

The full version of the Ten Commandments can be found in the book of Exodus 20: 2-17. Below is an abbreviated version:

1. Do not put other gods before me
2. Do not make or worship idols
3. Do not misuse the name of the Lord your God
4. Remember the Sabbath day by keeping it holy
5. Honor your father and your mother
6. Do not commit murder
7. Do not commit adultery
8. Do not steal
9. Do not lie
10. Do not covet your neighbor's things